T0122000

Heroin

The Rapids of My Life

OREN ELOW

iUniverse, Inc.
Bloomington

Heroin
The Rapids of My Life

iUniverse books may be ordered through booksellers or by contacting:

iUniverse
1663 Liberty Drive
Bloomington, IN 47403
www.iuniverse.com
1-800-Authors (1-800-288-4677)

ISBN: 978-1-4502-5822-7 (pbk)
ISBN: 978-1-4502-5824-1 (cloth)
ISBN: 978-1-4502-5823-4 (ebk)

Library of Congress Control Number: 2010913921

Printed in the United States of America

iUniverse rev. date: 12/3/2010

To my father Wesley Elow
my late friends Stanley Jones and A. C. Hillman
and to my late mentor Emeritus George K. Makechnie
dean of Sergent College at Boston University.

Contents

ONE

GROWING up in LOUISIANA

Mama, not only had an inner beauty, but a physical one as well. She was a Creole mulatto and her thick black hair hung just below her shoulders and under-curved at the tip. Her face was soft and round and her body classically shaped. If she had lived during the days of Michelangelo, she certainly would have been an ideal model for one of his great works of art.

Anyway, one morning after breakfast when I was it the fourth year of my birth, Mama and I were out in the backyard, and while she hung her clothes out in the sun to dry. I observed three men digging a hole in an unfenced empty lot near our home, which was juxtapose to my Aunt Daisy, and her husband Uncle Joe's home.

Being a child, I was full of curiosity. Thus, I asked Mama for what reason were they digging a hole in the ground. She always had an answer for me. While removing a few clothespins from a white canvas bag that hung from her shoulder, she pinned Daddy's blue work overalls to the clothesline and told me that they were digging for treasures.

"What's treasure?" I quizzed as I walked behind her in the cool, dew-damped grass—grass that Daddy had mowed last evening.

"Money," Mama answered, kicking off her house slippers to, also walk on the cool damp grass barefooted.

I guess that was the best answer she could give to a four-year-old, for even

I knew what money was. However, my inquisitive young mind wanted to know more. So I asked her where they looking for pennies or nickels. Mama smiled down at me with her lovely round yellowish, white face, free of make-up and continued hanging her wash under the large pecan trees.

Moreover, just as Mama had predicted early on, the three-men who had dug the hole in the ground for weeks, had found nothing. However, when they departed they left it uncovered, and it filled with water. Months later, though, I found out that the hole was at least twelve feet deep and twelve feet in diameter. In addition, I must say that both Mama and Daddy had counseled me on numerous occasions not to ever play in the empty lot, nor go near that hole.

On one of those sizzling days, when Mama and Daddy were at work and my sisters in school and the blazing sun weaves dance before me, I crossed the two cars, oyster-shell covered driveway, which separated our home, from the home of Aunt Daisy and Uncle Joe, and reported to Aunt Daisy who babysat me five days a week. Aunt Daisy was in her kitchen trying to repair, again, her old overused, broken down washing machine that had stopped working in the middle of her wash, saw me entered the kitchen through the screen door.

"I got lots of work to do today," she said to me, "and I want you to be good, Okay."

"Okay," I said, not knowing whether I should turn around and go back outside or just ignore her and hang around the kitchen as her two sons were doing.

Her youngest sons, Henry and Little Joe, curiously stood nearby in the kitchen watching their mother work on her washing machine while Anna Mae, the youngest of the daughters, wobbled on the kitchen floor in a tantrum. Boy, when she got to screaming, yelling, and rolling, around on the floor for her mother's attention, it seemed as though she would go on forever.

With the mayhem going on in the kitchen, an idea rush upon me like a hot flash. Hence, I eased out of the kitchen door pounce from the small porch to the ground and off I ran to the lot with the forbidden treasure hole and began playing near it. Picking up rocks and throwing them into the yellowish water; then, watching as the ripples spread like magic across the surface. As my courage assembled, I moved closer and closer to the edge of the forbidding hole. I felt comfortable and alert. Therefore, I sat down on its edge and tried placing my bear-feet into the water; however, my legs were too short. I tried stretching them to make them longer; instead, with the ease of sliding down a schoolyard sliding board, I smoothly slid off the wet edge into the water.

For some God given reason I did not go under. I just knew for some underlying principle that I would get myself out of this situation, and no one would ever know that I'd been there. Thus, I kicked my tiny feet and slapped my hands against the water to stay afloat. However, since I was near the water edge, I tried climbing out, only to slip right back down the yellowish-clay embankment into the water. After a few minutes, which seemed like hours in a child mind, I paddled away from the area I'd been trying to free myself, to an area where patches of grass grew. On my first try, I dug my fingerers into the roots of a patch of grass and pulled my body to safety.

For years, I'd quivered every time I thought of that incident, and ask myself where did a four-year old child, who'd never swim before, except in his mother's womb, get the courage and energy to stay afloat and fight for life without panicking. Why hadn't I drowned, or gone under? It was a miracle, and that wouldn't be the last miracle in my life.

My shorts were soaked-and-wet, and glued to my body. How would I get them to dry before Laura and Betty returned home from school, for lunch? Not only did I have to worry about getting them dried before they got home. I also had to worry about getting out of them, putting on a different pair and hope that Aunt Daisy wouldn't notice the change. However, I had to first by-pass her house, in order to reach our house.

I ran from the lot with athletic speed, with my bare chest hitting the heat waves until I reached my aunt's back porch. There I lowered myself on all four, so neither she nor my cousins would see me from the opened kitchen door. On hands and knees I moved to the end of the porch, lifted my head once again to make sure no one saw me. Thing were quit except for the old washing machine, which was now working and jerk, jerking away. With no eyes on me, I flew across the oyster-shell-covered driveway. Pounced onto our small back porch into the kitchen, and slid on the waxed linoleum floor into my sisters and I bedroom. There I pulled from one of the bureau's drawers a clean pair of shorts. Definitely nothing like the khaki ones, I wore to the treasure hole.

Outside on the back porch I scouted for a place to lay out my wet shorts to dry. The only thing on the porch was a tin washtub, which the family used for both bathing and clothes washing. Daddy never did get around to buying Mama a washing machine, nor did we have a built-in bathroom or electric refrigerator in the house, like Aunt Daisy and Uncle Joe had. Mama washed clothes on a scrubbing board, and we used the outhouse, in the back yard to alleviate ourselves. I laid the shorts on top of the over turned tub, not bothering to wring the water from them.

When I entered Aunt Daisy's kitchen she was standing over the stove cooking dinner and the boys were playing on the high waxed living room floor with their colorful race cars, while Anna Mae napped on the family room sofa, sucking her thumb. No one seemed to have missed me, nor noticed my change of shorts.

However, I wasn't so lucky when my sisters, Laura and Betty, returned home from school for noon's lunch. They could tell right off that something just wasn't right when they saw me waiting for them on the porch.

"Boy! Why your skin so chalky?" Betty bellowed, as I jumped from the porch to the ground in play.

"Oren!" Laura exclaimed, noticing my wet shorts sitting on top the tub. "Oren, you better not lie to us we can see you been in the waterhole!" She continued, pointing a finger toward the treasure hole. "I just know that's what you done!"

"Look at you!" Betty bawled. "Yeah, you been over there that's why you so chalky looking."

"Oh, shut up, y'all don't know nothing."

"We know you been in that hole! Who save you?" Laura said.

"Must be Aunt Daisy save him," Betty said.

"Nobody save me, I done it myself," I proudly said feeling like Superman.

"How come you didn't drown?" Betty uttered. "You don't know how to swim. So how you save yourself?"

"Will, I did! I know how to swim," I uttered and stormed into the house.

"Did you tell Aunt Daisy you fell in the hole?" Laura asked through the screen door.

"No."

"How about Henry and Little Joe, do they know?" Laura asked.

"No! Nobody saw me!" I said and began to cry. I had, had enough of their questioning. While Betty came into the house to make lunch, Laura rinsed out my shorts underneath the faucet, which set, juxtapose to the porch and placed them back on top of the tub to dry. She then called me back outside, washed me and made me promise that I'd never play near the hole again. I promised and stuck to it. No one ever said anything about that to Mama or Daddy. Afterward, we went into the house where Laura helped Betty prepare lunch.

Betty who had already gotten the lunchmeat out of the icebox told me to go into it and get the mayonnaise and soda water. The icebox sat in our bedroom. It was one of those huge solid oak iceboxes, in which every morning the iceman placed two large blocks of ice at its bottom to keep the food cold, and fresh.

I placed the items on the table and jumped onto one of the country chair. However, because I was still too small to eat sitting, I knelt on the chair to reach the tabletop. After lunch, Laura and Betty hurriedly tidied up the kitchen, escorted me to Aunt Daisy's and returned to school, along with Aunt Daisy's children whom had also returned home for dinner.

At noon Uncle Joe, who operated a giant crane for Conrad Brick Yard in New Iberia, the same yard my father drove tractor-trailer for, also came home for dinner. At that time of day, Daddy was on the road delivering bricks. For this reason, Mama cooked dinner in the evening after her domestic work hours.

Daddy had one sister and three brothers, and he and two of the brothers purchased a piece of land in New Iberia, Louisiana in the 1930s. In addition, on that land they each built their home side-by-side, to each other. Now, Nan, Daddy's sister built her home in Lafayette, which was a promising and growing oil town, some twenty miles west of New Iberia. Nan built the largest house of her siblings. Nonetheless, Daddy was the first to have a telephone installed. It was rare for African Americans in the mid 1940s to have such luxuries. Besides, I can still remember Mama teaching me how to use it so that I could reach her at work. I'd pick up the receiver; then, wait for the switchboard operator to answer. I'd give her the three digests, Mama taught me, and the operator, in return connected me to Mama's job; that's if the party line wasn't busy.

The Elow family worked hard for the things they owned. They were decedents of slave Grandparents, mill workers, and sharecroppers; yet they had managed to pull themselves out of the fields and mills and built their own homes in the growing cities.

Daddy was a handsome man about five feet ten, medium built, with a hard body, shaped and kept toned by hard work. In addition, he forever had a happy-go-lucky attitude across his brown face. He was also a great storyteller, who would take me upon his lap and tell me all kind of stories. My favorite was how he and Uncle Joe, who was a little taller than Daddy and looked Native American, were friends of Santa Claus. Just before midnight, on Christmas Eve, Daddy said that Santa Claus would pick him and Uncle Joe up on the railroad tracks, which was pitch-black and fogged in.

He said that if it wasn't for the bright red light, radiating from the nose of Rudolph the Red Nose Reindeer, it wouldn't have been possible to land the jingle-bell sleigh on the dark and foggy tracks. The two brothers would then climb on board, and off they flew, high into the moon lighted, star bright sky, with Rudolph the Red Nose Reindeer leading the way. Daddy and Uncle Joe's only job was to push Santa's down chimneys that were too narrow for his jolly, holly plump figure. With the gifts all delivered Santa would find a great white fluffy cloud, lighted by a full silvery moon to park his jingle-bell sleighs. There the three of them feasted on milk and cookies left for Santa by the children. After they had eaten their snacks, Santa drop the brothers off, again, on the dark railroad tracks, with a, "Ho, ho, ho; and a Merry Christmas to all." I would ask Daddy how long it took them to pass out all the presents.

"Oh, about one hour," he'd smiled and began another story to avoid my questions.

My father and Uncle Joe were more than just brothers they were best friends. On weekends, the two spent their time along the railroad tracks drinking in saloons with sawdust floors. In addition, on occasions, they'd frequently created scenes, by either starting fights with their contemporaries inside the saloons or picking on people on their way home.

They say the only reason Daddy and Uncle Joe got away with fighting and agitating White people in the neighborhood, when they were drinking was, because the Elow family was under the protection of Mr. Conrad, the man whom employed both Daddy and Uncle Joe.

Thus, because of his status and a lifelong resident of New Iberia and a prominent businessperson people, black and white, listened when Mr. Conrad spoke. Even the law listened to him, though he was no taller than Napoleon. It was also said by the dead and gone and the still living that the Elow family and the Conrad Cajun clan are part of the same bloodline. All I knew at age four was that I liked Mr. Conrad, and that he always treated our extended family with great civility.

Daddy went from drinking on weekends, to drinking almost daily. Therefore, there came a time when he wouldn't get up out of bed in the morning for work, unless Mr. Conrad came by the house in early morning, just before dawn and awakened him. Most mornings I'd hear Mr. Conrad when he came tapping on Mama and Daddy's bedroom window.

"Wesley, Wesley, get up. We got to work today."

Daddy would crawl out of bed, wash his face in cold water, whether winter or summer, rejuvenate himself with a cup of freshly made coffee, spooned with sugar. So much sugar that portions of it remained at the cup's bottom. We kids loved to finger lick the sweet from the coffee cups, after the grown-ups had finished. However, finger licking the cake bowls were even better.

The more my father got involved in alcoholism, the more he lacked consideration for himself, and respect for his family. The first fight I experienced between my parents happened one evening while we were at the kitchen table preparing for dinner. Daddy had come home tipsy, and he and Mama began arguing over who knows what. Moreover, and like out nowhere Mama got hold of a jar of Noxzema, and throws it at Daddy who stood near the kitchen's back door talking trash. The jar missed him, and smashed against the door, sending Noxzema flying all over the walls and floor; thus robbing the kitchen from the aroma of Creole cooking, and replacing it with the scent of face cream.

My sisters and I were fortunate that our dinner was still on the stove in their covered pots. Daddy, not knowing what Mama might throw next; swiftly exit the kitchen through the back door, as if he was Speedy Gonzales. Mama fixed our plates and sent us into her bedroom to eat while she washed down the kitchen.

Daddy had probably gone next door to his brother, Uncle Morris's home; and when he returned, Mama and I were sitting on the sofa in the front room listing to the radio. Laura and Betty were in our bedroom giggling and jumping on the bed as if it were a trampoline.

My father entered the house through the front door and as he passed us on his way to their bedroom, the two not so much as glanced at one another or said a word. I had great love for both my mother and father; hence, I never picked sides, for they were equal in my mind.

Before Mama put me to bed, I asked her for a nickel so that in the morning, I'd go just around the corner from our house, to Mr. and Mrs. Roy's miniature grocery store and buy a bag of penny candy or cookies. Sweets were my first addiction. Mama told me to go into their bedroom and take a nickel from Daddy's pants pocket. In my petite mind, I felt that this was wrong and hesitated.

"Go on," she insisted, assuring me with a grin written across her lovely face, that it was all right. I got down from the sofa and went into their room where only a silhouette of light coming in from the front room guided me to the wooden chair that daddy had thrown his overalls across. I then reached into the pocket with the coins, feeling like a thief in the night. As I stuck my hand into the pocket, I heard Daddy's voice, which startled me and almost made me wet my underwear.

"Oren! Get out of my pockets," he said, moving around in the bed, which made me think he was getting up to give me a whipping. "Don't you know that's stealing?" he complained. I was too ashamed to say a word and left the room feeling like a puppy, yelled at for pooping in the house.

"Wesley!" Mama yelled. "I told him it was okay."

"It's not okay!" he shouted back.

As I climbed back onto the sofa in my shame, I could no longer hear my sisters playing in the bedroom and I guessed like me, they were praying, *please God don't let them fight again.* A few minutes later, we could hear Daddy snoring.

TWO

Mama, Breakfast and my Nickel

The next morning I got up and went into the kitchen where, on the kitchen table sat a milky-white cereal bowl half filled with cornflakes. Also on the table, next to a milky-white bowl, to my surprise, was a gleaming nickel, no doubt left by Mama. As a result, every morning thereafter, when I awoke my nickel was right there on the table along with my breakfast. Nor Laura or Betty hadn't awakened me before leaving for school. Hell, what seven and nine-year olds want to be bothered with their little brother on a school day.

From the icebox, I took a quart glass-bottle of milk to the table, climbed upon a chair and poured some into the bowl of cornflakes; then, returned the milk to the icebox. Afterward, I ate my breakfast where my gleaming nickel and I smiled at one another; I could already feel the excitement of the day anxiously moving through me. For I was a kid who adored playing games; and wanted to do just that, get out and play. At age four I could do, in play, what twelve year olds did; fight, shoot marbles, spin tops, climb trees … and most schoolyard games. I'd no problem playing with other kids, in fact I enjoyed it, nonetheless, sometimes, I liked playing alone.

When I finished breakfast, I was on my way out the kitchen door to report to Aunt Daisy, at same time the iceman was entering the door carrying a large block of ice with a pair of tongs. The block of ice was wrapped in a piece of heavy clothe to control the melting.

Hoping to get a few pennies from the iceman to go with my nickel, I held the kitchen screen door open for him. The iceman looked down at me with his tiny blue eyes and his farmer-tanned face, and asked me in Creole how was I doing. Almost everyone spoke Creole—black and white. Aunt Daisy would have to wait, for my forever-meddlesome mind took over. I was one of those kids who believed that I could learn by watching. Therefore, most time when the iceman came by, I'd be right there looking over his shoulders as he repeated his routine every other morning. He'd pull from his back pocket a piece of rag and wiped up drips of water that had fallen to the floor as he placed the first block of ice, in its proper place, at the bottom of the icebox.

I followed the iceman to his ice-truck for the second and last block of ice. Moreover, when he opened the rear shutter to the refrigerated truck, a cool breeze, carried by a rush of frosty vapor, escaped the opened compartments that was stack with blocks of ice, and quenches the morning heat.

After he placed the last block of ice in the icebox he, again, removed the rag from his back pocket and wiped the drips of water from the floor near the icebox. Thereafter, we left the house together.

On the back porch as the iceman was leaving I said, "Iceman, can I have a penny?"

He placed both tongs and heavy cloth on top of the washtub, dug into his damp pocket, and pulled out a fist full of coins. He picked out three pennies and gave them to me. Now I had eight cent, I was rich. I thanked the iceman, as I jumped from the porch onto the ground and ran straight over to Mr. and Mrs. Roy's store before reporting to Aunt Daisy. The Roy's store was just around the corner and there was no street to cross. Nevertheless, that wouldn't have stopped me I was use to crossing the streets alone.

In our back yard, not far from the clothesline, was Mama's garden, where daddy had once buried my baby-bottle with my permission. I was almost five, then, and still nursing a bottle. It wasn't a thing, but when I wanted it and didn't get it, I'd go into a crying mess: Yelling and screaming until I got it. Over the past few months, both parents tried through all types of bribes hoping that I'd give it up—like buying me small toys and candies; but none of those things worked.

In the yard, I played near Daddy as he stacked lumber to build an addition to the house. As I played and he worked, he spoke to me about giving up my bottle. He claimed that if I gave it to him he'd plant it right there in

Mama's garden and from it a large corn stalk, where heads of sweet yellow corn would grow just all in one night. Daddy knew that I enjoy eating boiled corn and he figure that perhaps, I'd give my bottle, to him, for some sweet boiled corn. He was right, and caught me in a good mood. I always felt good in Daddy's present.

Saturday, the next morning, I awoke Daddy who had the smell of rotten alcohol on his breath from, "last night." Daddy got out of bed and put on his overalls snapping one of the straps across his bare chest. Moreover, before going outside, he stopped at the icebox, poured him an ice-cold glass of water, and drunk it down, as though his guts were on fire. Outside he went over to the side of the porch, turned on the water faucet, washed his face in his hands, and goggling his mouth with water.

As we near the head of the garden Daddy came to an abrupt stop and roared, "There it is, there it is!" he uttered, pointing to the back of the garden. The cornstalk as Daddy had promised had grown over night like Jack and the beanstalk.

We both, without delay moved throw the furrow row—I first. There, Daddy reached for the corn stalk and broke off one of the three heads of corn, and shucked it halfway. He then poked his thumbnail into a few kernels, and their yellow juices popped out.

"See!" Daddy blurted, showing me his thumbnail covered with sweet corn juice. "I told you so!"

However, when I'd grown a little older, and knew just how corn cultivated, I knew he'd outsmarted me. He could have gotten the cornstalk at any garden or farm in the area and buried it in Mama's garden. Nevertheless, he'd done what he's set out to do, burry my bottle. This was just another story for him to tell.

Even with his advance-drinking problem, Daddy tried not to neglect his children. There were times in the afternoon after returning home from work; he'd get down in the dirt, on his hands and knees, and play marble with myself and some of the neighborhood kids. I loved being his son, for he constantly found ways to make me feel like his little man.

On occasions, he'd take me on some of his job sight. At one of those job sight, Daddy warned me not to play in the area where there sat a mammoth greasy pipe that was on the lot, on which he stacked his load of bricks. The pipe was round and gigantic enough for me to walk upright and stretch out my arms without touching either walls or ceiling.

As the morning passed into lunch and then into afternoon, Daddy still had many, more stacks of bricks on the truck to unload. I passed the morning playing in the shade underneath a large tree. After we had eaten lunch, he returned to his unloading.

When the sun reached my tree of play, Daddy had me moved to the shade near the enormous pipe, large enough a car could roll through it. I looked into the pipe and thought that just maybe I could walk straight through it, to the other end without getting, no more than my bare feet greasy. Dark-brown grease caked the floor and walls of the pipe; yet I felt I could walk it without getting any on my clothes.

I stuck my head into the pipe as if I were some kind of pipe investigator. I slowly move in to it and, right off, I almost slipped in the grease beneath my feet. However, I quickly recovered my steadiness, and slowly gaited forward. In addition, the more I stepped forward, the harder it became for me to balance myself and by midway, I'd already slipped and fallen a few times; and by the time I reached the other side, I looked like an oil driller.

When Daddy laid eyes on me, he looked at me in a state of distress. He didn't know whether to yell at me, spank me, or laugh—maybe even cry. What he did do is clean me off the best way he knew how. He knew that water was out of the question, it would have only made matters worst. It would be like trying to wash a greasy dish in cold water. Therefore, he gently rubbed my arms and legs, my bare chest and short pants with masonry sand that was already on the lot. Then, took his railroad-handkerchief from his back pocket and whipped the sand and grease from my body. However, I was still grimy.

We arrived home late in the afternoon and in play, Daddy opened the screen door and pushed me into the kitchen, where Mama stood before the stove cooking dinner. I tried sliding back behind him, but he used his whole body and blocked me.

"Oh no, let your mother see what you look like," Daddy said, easing me back if front of Mama.

"Boy—she exclaimed," looking similar to the animated woman character on the Tom and Jerry show, apron tied around her waist, oversize house slippers on her feet, spoon in hand, and full of authority.

"Oren?" Mama exclaimed! "What did you get in to, this time? Just look at you, boy! Just look at you!"

"Lord, Wesley, what you let the boy get into?" Mama quarreled. "You know you got to keep an eye on him; like he got ants in the pants, or something."

Daddy tried explaining what happened; however, he would have done better if he'd spoken to the water in the wash-pan sitting on the wash-table awaiting him. Because Mama, after a hard day's work, didn't want to hear it.

Mama, it the meantime, prepared supper for Daddy and the girls; then, took me by the hand onto the porch. Moreover, from the faucet she filled a large cooking pot with water and went back into the house, where she placed it on the stove. When the water was hot enough, Mama came back onto the porch, where I was now spinning my yellow top, poured the hot water into the washtub, and then added water from the faucet to cool it. Back into the house, she went again, and this time exited carrying a few pieces of rags, a bar of homemade soap and washed me until I was screechy clean.

When finished washing me, Mama and went into the house where both Daddy and my sisters had finished eating, and Mama fixed both her and me dinner. Daddy had gone to his room to read the daily newspaper, while Laura and Betty were in their room doing their homework.

However, as Mama and I were eating, Daddy playfully eased into the kitchen from his room joking about what I looked like when he first saw me greasy.

"Oh, hush Wayway," Mama said, now in a better frame of mind. "The boy came home looking like something out a funny book." Everybody burst in to laughter, for now Laura and Betty had made it into the kitchen. When Mama was in a good mood, she called Daddy, Wayway. It was his nickname for spending more time in saloons along the railroad tracks; Than he did at home.

The next morning when I woke up, my nickel as usual was on the kitchen table. After having finished breakfast, and before going over to check in with Aunt Daisy, I went around the corner to Mr. and Mrs. Roy's store a bought a package of the gingerbread cake, the kind covered with pink frosting. Mr. and Mrs. Roy were warm-hearted people, who were in their mid sixties; yet they still had smooth, glowing reddish-skin and the hair on their head soft, straight and silvery.

That afternoon when Daddy had returned home from work, he brought with him one of Mr. Conrad's pick-up trucks. Whenever he brought one of those trucks home, it meant only one thing, the family was going crab fishing the next morning.

On Saturday morning, we all piled into the truck. Betty sat on Laura's lap and Laura sat between Daddy and Mama, while I stood between Mama's legs holding onto the dashboard, and stared out the window, at the gravel road and farmland on either side.

When we arrived at Morgan City, Mama and the girls crab fished from the beach of the Atlantic Ocean while Daddy took me on board a small boat for some reason or another. I felt quite apprehensive being on the boat. I didn't like the feeling of the boat dancing on the rough tide beneath my feet. For I knew enough to understand that the, sea is unlike the water hole I'd fallen in.

We left the boat, and that wasn't too soon for me, and returned to the spot where Mama and my sisters were fishing. We joined them, and by time we left the beach of the Gulf of Mexico, we had caught at least a bushel of crabs. Moreover, that night with the presence of Uncle Joe, Uncle Morris and their families, we had a boiled crab feast.

The yard's lighting, which hung just below the peak of the house roof, illuminated the porch and a portion of the back yard. Two smoky fires, burning in barrels placed on either side of the yard curb harassing misquotes. Next to the porch set, a long rustic wood table covered with dishes of crabs. While the grown-ups sat at the table cracking crabs and drinking beer and wine: Laura and Betty along with Aunt Daisy's daughters, Ethel and Mary Ann, played hopscotch, as moths and bugs flew over head in the beam of the house light. On the other hand Henry and me played cowboy and Indian, while little Joe spent most of the night at Aunt Daisy's side or sitting on her knees.

The summer past gracefully and Christmas, my favorite day of the year, was just a few hours away; and Mama, the girls and me enjoyed ourselves in the front room decorating our tabletop size Christmas tree, near an un-curtained window, facing the road. We fully decorated it with ornaments, colorful lights, icicles and angel hair, too. Moreover, a little angel figurine rested on the tree's peak. After decoration, we all cuddled on the sofa, enjoying the tree and listening to Christmas carols on the radio, while awaiting Daddy to come home.

When Daddy came home, drunk, he and Mama immediate got in to an argument. The argument was so fiery, that either Mama or Daddy took our charming Christmas tree, open the front door, and tossed the tree, outside, onto the graveled road.

I couldn't believe what my sisters and were witnessing, for everything seemed to be moving at super-speed. This wasn't supposed to happen, this was a time for kids and toys.

My entire body felt as if I were a melting candle. Yet I didn't lose hope, I wanted to believe that either Mama or Daddy would go out in a minute, and rescue our joyful Christmas tree. I didn't care about any damages. I just wanted it back on the table. However, to my yearning no one stepped out into the Christmas night to retrieve it. That night became one of the darkest nights in my young life. Moreover, I do believe this is when my delinquent behavior began.

A few months after Christmas I woke up one morning, found the house empty and no nickel or breakfast, sat, on the table. I immediate sense something dreadfully wrong. Laura and Betty were in school and Daddy at work. However, the whereabouts of Mama worried me deeply, for she had never forgotten to leave both breakfast and nickel on the kitchen table when she left, for work, in the mornings. I ran out the house to that of my aunt's crying and inquiring about Mama's whereabouts.

Aunt Daisy took one look at my quivering and took me in her arms, assuring me, "Your mama's at work," then advised me to go home and call her.

I dashed out of her house, ran back home and into Mama and Daddy's room. I went to the phone sitting on one of the end tables and gave the operator the three digests, and she connected me to Miss. Hall's line, the woman whom Mama worked for; however, there was no answer. That when I knew that Mama had indeed left use, and knew that she would not be coming back.

Hence, I spent the whole morning crying. When Laura and Betty returned home for lunch, they didn't know any more than I did about Mama's whereabouts; and it wasn't until Daddy came home that evening, that the families learned that Mama wasn't coming back. I guessed that Mama had had enough of Daddy's drunken behavior. Nevertheless, how could she leave me after spoiling and loving me so dearly? Why I cried night after night, why?

If the experience with Mama's leaving wasn't enough, the real shocker came when I learned that, Mama, wasn't our real mother, after all, but rather our stepmother. That Daddy and, Marjorie his first wife, our biological mother had divorced eight months after I was born.

This whole episode took me some time to get over, especially Mama not being around anymore to mollycoddle me. She had been the warmth of my life. When I did happen to see Mama again, I was eight years old and living in Lafayette. She'd come by the schoolyard during noon reset where I played with some of my class mates to say hello. Miss. Grace, we now called her, looked sadden and her mulatto face showed signs of aging. She had gained some weight and looked shorter than when I knew her, perhaps that because I was taller.

Nevertheless, she was still a handsome woman and seeing her brought back the blissful times I'd spent with her. She only stayed a few minutes, and though our conversation was drought ridden, it was friendly. After that visit, I never saw Mss. Grace Mouton again.

With Mama gone, I soon became very attached to Daddy, not that I wasn't already. In addition, whenever he got into his 1945 blue Ford to go anywhere without me, I'd go into a crying, screaming fit of temper, for I didn't want to see him go for fear of never seeing him again.

One winter day with pecans falling, from giant pecan trees, onto the houses tin rooftop my sister and I were home alone. We were playing in Daddy's bedroom, which was quite spacious. In the center of the room sat a large gas heather, and to keep warm the three of us played around it. We were having an abundant of fun before Laura bumped into me causing me to fall on the heather; thus, burning the right side of my neck. No sooner, had my neck hit the top of the hot surface of the heather, I began crying, no, yelling. Poor Laura, she was so afraid that she wet herself, something she sometime did when anxious.

My burnt neck certainly couldn't be kept from Daddy, and this bothered Laura and Betty; they both feared a whipping when Daddy got home. Laura gently tried rubbing homemade butter on my burn; however, one touch of her hand sent burning pains throughout my entire body. Somehow, through sobs and sniffles, she tenderly rubbed the butter over the burn; then, wrapped a white cloth around it. While Laura bandaged me, Betty stood over her biting softly at her inner wrist; a habit Betty developed to ease her anxiety. Laminating, I climbed onto Daddy's bed and mourned for hours.

Because of racism and the lack of money, few blacks went to the hospital. It was the healers, the layers of hands, and the midwife, who were mostly involved in the community doctoring. In my situation, Laura played doctor because no one was going over to Aunt Daisy's to report my agony. My sisters felt that they were in enough trouble with daddy—they were not only afraid—they felt terrible about my condition.

When Daddy got home, I was standing in the kitchen's doorway waiting for him while Laura and Betty sat quietly on the floor before the heater. As soon as Daddy opened the door and saw me, he noticed my runny nose and my face wet with tears. Most likely, he thought that I was crying for him to return home. It wasn't until he had removed his work handkerchief from his pants' back pocket and stooped to wipe my face that he noticed the cloth wrapped around my neck. Daddy closed the door behind him as he entered the kitchen and lifted me up.

"Boy! Where you get this greasy rag around your neck from; playing cowboy and Indian," he joked, holding me in one arm and untied the cloth with the other.

However, before he touches me I began crying, "It hurt it hurt! "

"What hurt? Let me see," and screech when he saw the pink flesh and the burn. "Oren! Oren! He exclaims what you got into?"

One thing about Daddy, whether sober or drunk, he never spanked his children, nor had I ever seen him put his hands on Mama. However, that day, after washing my neck and giving me a bath, dressed my burn with yellowish petroleum and wrapping it in clean gauzes. He did spank Laura, hitting more of her dress than her behind, with his leather belt. Nevertheless, Laura yelled as if she was being slaughter.

Right after my neck incident, I guessed Daddy knew working long hours and having an alcohol problem, he could no longer rear us. Therefore, one day, in 1949, he packed us into his car with some belongings and drove us to Lafayette to live with his sister, Nan.

THREE

MOVING in with DADDY'S SISTER

Nan was a small woman in her mid sixties with a root-beer complexion and long silvery hair, which she always set in a donut, covered either, with a kerchief or starched bonnet. In addition, Nan's small frame still had a fair shape to it, and men still admired her arresting legs.

I liked the idea living with Nan and living in one of the largest houses in the neighborhood. When my sisters and I moved in with her, my tantrums stop whenever daddy left me and climbed into his car. Daddy continued living in New Iberia and would visit us on weekends with money and groceries.

Nan was already taking care of three of her grandchildren when we moved in: Joan and her sister, Janelle, who were the daughters of Cousin Francis and Cousin Bell. Arthur Roy, whose mother and father, Cousin Freddie and Cousin Lucile, lived only across the graveled road from Nan's house, also lived with Nan. In addition, there was a young woman, in her early twenty, who lived in the house as well. She was quite attractive with a Hershey's brown complexion and a well-proportioned body. Nuzie was her name, and she was a close relative of Nan's deceased husband.

Cousin Lucile was a big woman about six feet and weighed all of two hundred pounds; with brown skin and a round serious face, which she often used to pretend her toughness. It worked, because in her present I was very careful of what I did or said, fearing a slap upside the head. Something she never did. She never laid her hands on me, or my sisters.

Many the older people, in those days, used either face expressions or vocal tone to make children behave. That's not to say they wouldn't use their hands, switches, ropes, extension cords, to get at that ass if children were misbehaving.

In August 1949, on the first morning of school opening, Cousin Lucile took us to school; including her children Malcolm, Geraldine, and Jerry. We were all bright and fresh in our new school uniforms, looking like a painting done by Normal Rockwell, with my Cousin Lucile leading the pack. Walking tall, her big bosom pushed forward, and her sizeable *derrière* flopped from side-to-side.

The streets radiated with both black and white kids, dressed in their newly attire or uniforms. Like me some of them too, were going to school for the first time. The difference, though, black kids were going to Colored schools only, and white kids were going to White schools only.

I felt a since of joy being with the other kids on our way to school; however, fear as well posted itself among my joy. Nevertheless, there I finally was, walking to school with Cousin Lucile holding onto my hand. I really was looking forward to it. However, when my cousin tried passing me over to the kindergarten nun in charge of my kindergarten class. I forthwith exploded into a tantrum, screaming, jumping up and down, and trying to pull my cousin to the floor with me. If I thought, I could pull her down to the floor with me I got nowhere. In fact, with her grip and strength, not even my knees touch the floor.

Just then, the nun took hold of me, "Come Oren, I've the perfect seat for you," she said in a stiff voice, while she gently with authority wrapped her strong fingers around my wrist and patiently removed me from the backside of Cousin Lucile, where I'd locked my arm around one of her fleshy thighs.

"No! I want to go home!" I snapped, while trying in vain to pull my wrist free from the nun's mighty hold, all the time awaiting a slap across the cranium by my cousin, which never came. Moreover, the nun, perhaps, would not have been offend, if my cousin had wacked me.

The nun was also a large woman, as large as Cousin Lucile, and when she looked down on me who now wiggled at her side. I could see authority written all over her pale white face, which resembled a Chinese theatre mask, tucked into a black and white habit. The nun pulled me so close to her that my face pressed against her large black Rosary beads, which hung from her hip. I could also smell the incense the church burns coming from her full-length black habit.

It seemed as though all nuns and priests, too, at Saint Paul had this smell coming from their clothing. It wasn't at all offensive to me. It smelled like Catholic Church, a smell I deeply appreciate to this day. To me the smell of incense gives the Catholic Church, the priests and the nuns a sense of holiness.

I was one happy kid when Friday arrived, for Nan had promised me that if I behave myself in school she'd let me go to the country for the weekend. That Friday evening, Cousin Francis, one of Nan's four sons, and his wife Cousin Bell came to visit Nan as they so often did.

Moreover, that night when they departed for their, sharecropping, farm in Church Point, they took me, and their daughter, Janelle back to the country with them.

On Saturday morning, only Cousin Francis went out into the cotton field to work a half day as most farmers did on Saturdays. Cousin Bell caught up on her chores around the house, cleaning and washing; including feeding her chickens and working in her garden, while Janelle and I played kickball on the dusty headland in front of the house.

At noon, after Cousin Francis retired from the field, we all took a bath; then, drove to Duson. Duson was a little town some five miles south of Church Point, and twenty miles west of Lafayette, with a population of about seven hundred people.

On our way to Duson, Janelle and I sat in the back seat looking out the car windows of my cousin Francis, 1949 blue Ford. Because it was Saturday, there were more people than usually traveling the blacktop highway, which led to Duson. Some were traveling in cars, others in buggies.

As we past them on other either side, either Cousin Francis or Cousin Bell would wave to them, whether they were black or white persons. I cannot remember any white farmers whom we didn't get along with, though some were racist. Everyone knew each other, spoke the same French Creole, and at one time or another had helped, each other work their land. I irrupted playing with Janelle so that I wouldn't miss seeing Nan's old farmhouse, where she and her family once lived and sharecropped.

Janelle spoke before I could get a word out, "Look! It's Nan's old house!"

"Yeah, that old house done got weather beat," Cousin Bell, said. "Yeah, it's old. Just look at it. Just sitting there in them tall grass, looking like a picture."

No one had lived in the house since Nan and her family had moved to Lafayette a few years earlier. In addition, the green grass, which shimmied in the soft summer breeze, under a solid blue-sky, and a red fireball sun bending in the west, had grown tall, making the weathered gray farmhouse, with its rusty tin roof, and dilapidated barn, out back, a museum painting.

"Look! Look!" Janelle uttered, pulling me from my museum piece, "Buffalos!"

In a pasture across the asphalt road from the Nan's old house, was a small group of buffalos, grazing alongside a heard of white Brahma bulls. Cousin Francis went on to explain to me and Janelle, the large white house on the other side of the pasture was the home, which belonged to the white landowners, who Nan and her family had sharecropped for, for years. This was the Jim Crow south, the days when blacks were still sharecropping and the burning of crosses by the Ku Klux Klan spelled Black hate, and Black men and women hung from trees, were terrorism absolute.

Therefore, if black people wanted to make a living, they had to take what jobs the white man placed aside for them; and most of the jobs were the same backbreaking jobs that they held down during slavery. Thus, some blacks took jobs as sharecroppers, while other work in the mills and other slave labor jobs. Nan's family did both, they either sharecropped or worked in the mills. However, they were the lucky ones, like my father and his family who by hard work and wits managed to save enough money to build their own homes and owned cars. Cousin Francis was the last of the family member to move into the city, as late as the 1970s.

We turned off the road, drove around a short exit curved, and enter Duson. Where the first thing we saw was an old gas station sitting as if it were a community guard-post. Cousin Francis pulled into the gas station where old junk cars filled the small lot. Stacked against the sidewalls, of the rundown, shotgun built shack, which the attendant used for both gas station and home, was stacks of empty, rusty, crude oil drums. Moreover, Coke Cola signs, Chesterfield, Lucky Strike, Camel, and Philip Morris cigarettes signs cluttered the station's front walls.

Cousin Francis got out of the car and stretched his six-foot farm and his earth-tone face glowed in the evening sunset. Furthermore, whether he was dressed in his farm rags or his Sunday best, he stood out. He was a handsome man and knew it, and so did the women. Well, he was a lady's man. So was my daddy.

The white proprietor of the gas station/home, wearing a greasy baseball cap pulled low revealing his leather looking face, stepped out the dingy shack; and forthwith, he and my cousin began a friendly conversation in Creole. They were old friends. Nan and her family had lived right down the road from the gas station, and the two had grown up together.

Most of the times I was confused when trying to understand why White people hated Black people. However, most White Cajuns and Black Creoles got along like family. Nevertheless, some White Cajun speaking Creoles were right out racist. Nan had warned us to be cautious of most White people.

I got out of the car parked next to the red gasoline pump. It was one of those old pumps, where station attendant had to first pump the gasoline from the pump into a large glass jar at the top of the tank. The jar was empty, thus I took hold of the red handle and pumped up gasoline into the jar. With the jar filled with gasoline, Cousin Francis ordered his usual, one-buck worth.

The tall and thin man with the greasy baseball cap removed the hose from the pump, with stain and grubby hands, worn from years of working on cars and pumping gas, and placed it into the car's gas tank. His fingernails and the tips of his fingers were creaked so bad that I couldn't tell whether they'd been bleeding or just grimy.

After leaving the shack my cousin dropped Cousin Bell, Janelle and me off at the home of one of their long time friend and went off to party at the only black folk's "juke joint" in Duson. While Cousin Bell and her obese, jaundice complexion friend, with stockings knotted at the knee, sat on the front screened porch conversing. Janelle and I went out doors, to play with a hand full of neighborhood kids playing catch ball in the middle of the dusty graveled road.

The next morning, we all put on our Sunday best and drove to Duson to attend nine o' clock Mass. As I found out, every Sunday the little white painted, Catholic Church filled every pew with standing room only. After

Mass while grown folks stood outside the church vocalizing on how good or bad their harvest would be that year. We children played tag as we ran through the crowd. The church was a place where neighborhoods met once a week for both spiritual enlightenment and community. So every Sunday, after Mass, they'd gathered in the church's yard and chirper among themselves for half hour or so. They spoke quickly to one other in Creole, hoping to express, in a half hour, all that had gone on in their lives that past week. Then as if a shotgun blast had gone off, they all scattered in their own direction.

However, we drove to Nan house in Lafayette; and that afternoon after dinner, like every Sunday afternoon, my cousin and best friend Jerry and I got together and went to the movies to see a double feature with two cartoons. I saw no sense in going to the movies if there were no cartoons. To children, cartoons and the Three Stooges were the icing on the features; it prepared the moviegoers for a great western or a King Kong.

Early the next morning I heard Nan moving about the house getting herself ready to attend six o'clock Mass. Every morning, seven days a week she went to Mass. Moreover, five of those days when she returned home, she would wake us up, cooked breakfast, and send us off to school.

On my way to school that morning, I ran into a few of my seven grade classmates who were walking the railroad track, on their way to school, so we hooked up and walked the rest of the way to together. Both Charles and Larry, two handsome mulatto brothers with straight blond hair talked of the new bikes their father had just bought for them. Also presented was Chip another mulatto. However, he had a bit of a jaundice tone to his skin than the brothers, and his hair, which he wore in a short round Afro, was coarse and brown. However, the brothers could pass for white, while Chip couldn't.

When I returned home from school that after noon Nan and some of our nearby neighbors all set in a circle in the living room. In the center of the circle was a large colorfully quilt that they had begun quilting. On the floor next to each of the six quilters' chairs were piles of colorful scrap of materials—mostly red and blue—which they had saved over the months for this very occasion, to make a beautiful country quilt. I could tell from their stitching and the weight of the cloths, on the floor, that the quilt was going to be tick and heavily made. Since the quilt was being quilter in Nan's house the quilt would, belongs to Nan.

In the kitchen, Laura sat at the kitchen table doing her homework; Thus, I thought I'd ask her a question that had been toying at my intellect. I asked her why Black people had so many skin colors.

"It has a lot to do with slavery," she responded without lifting her head from her book. I'd heard about slavery; however, I had no understanding of it, yet.

"Why, we got to sit in the back of the bus—"

"Stop asking me all those questions. I can't think!" Laura snapped.

Nan would forever warn us that when we got on the city bus to always go to the back of the bus to be seated. "You don't want trouble with no white folks about no seat," she counseled us in Creole. "Some of them can be so mean and some of them can be so good, too."

To keep me out of trouble, perhaps even from getting hurt or worst, Nan, each summer, during school vacation sent me off to my cousin farm where she felt I'd be safe from the grips of racist and malicious white men. I was a fresh kid and full of ideas and she thought the two might get me in trouble, so off I'd go to Cousin Francis' farm. Moreover, she felt by sending me to the farm it would give my cousin another hand to assist him in the fields. Nan didn't worry too much about the White Cajun Creole, harming Black Creole people; she had as many white friends as black ones.

However, In Lafayette Parish I can't recall any trouble between black and white. Maybe it was because they spoke the same languish, French Creole, or perhaps it was because they didn't know who they were, Cajuns or Creoles brothers or sisters. Therefore, they learned how to support and live next door to each other with very little fuss. Today I still have an immense love for my Creole roots and for the Creole and Cajun people of Louisiana, especially Lafayette Parish, the Creole/Cajun capital of the Pelican State.

FOUR

LIVING in BOSTON with my NEW FAMILY

In September of 1960, I moved to Boston to live with my biological mother and my stepfather. Mother was a plump little woman with a smooth, caramel, complexion and a babe face that always smiled at you. I was ,then, age sixteen, and I will never forget that long tiresome Greyhound bus ride hugging the East coast as it rolled on from Lafayette to Mississippi, and on through Alabama and Georgia, through the Carolinas; and on and on through New York City, the small state of Rhode Island, and finally, to Boston. I swore that I'd never do that kind of a ride again.

Boston was a new and strange land to me, big and metropolitan. Moreover, the buildings' architectural designs were much different from what I grow up seeing; but I liked very much what I saw.

Mother lived in a large spacious apartment, in Roxbury, with a lengthy corridor that began at the front door entrance and ended at the kitchen's threshold. In the living room, which looked like a magazine picture, cut into the upper corner wall, was a small stained-glass window, in floral design. The colors of the stained glass: ruby along with emerald, purple, blue, and gold, or yellow certainly brought back visions of the Catholic Church and its tall stained-glass widows.

Later I found out that stand-glass windows were a common thing in Boston homes.

Moreover, most of the Victorian built houses in Roxbury and elsewhere, in the city had them. These Victorian homes, treasured built with ceramic fireplaces, high ceilings, laurel crown moldings and hardwood floors, French doors, and elegant oak staircases. I liked the feel of Boston. I liked the feelings of its age, and that both Benjamin Franklin and Paul Revere had lived here. It's as if their spirit were still in the sphere of Boston.

Jesse, Mother's husband, was a little person, pleasant and generous, about five-foot five, with light complexion, dark brown wavy hair; and worked as a custodian at the Christian Science Church/Headquarter, on Massachusetts Avenue, in Boston. However, when he wasn't working, he could have been found at Suffolk Downs Race Track, playing the horses; or joking with his friends at the Baby Tiger Boxing Gym, playing the daily numbers and— drinking whiskey straight. Jesse was an Old Grand Dad's man.

Anyway, within a week Mother got me a job working at MIT, Massachusetts Institute of Technology, washing dishes, in one of their fraternities at Beacon Street. In addition, in the evenings, after work, I'd stop in at Frank's Poolroom on Humboldt Avenue, in Roxbury. A block away from home, to play pool and hang out with my cousin Jim and his friends, who were a few years older than I. Jim, was my first cousin and brotherly like, whom Mother had brought up to Boston, from New Iberia, years before I arrived. Though I really didn't know much about Mother, I certainly didn't like the idea that Jim had come to live in Boston before me and that she had made it possible, for him.

Nevertheless, in September 1960, Mother did come to my aid when she came to Lafayette to speak with the judge who had sent me, and two friends to reform school for breaking into a gas station and ripping off the money from Coke and cigarette machines. While sending me to reform school for these crimes the judge also charged me with running away from home. Mother asked the judge to release me in her custody and she'd take me back to Boston to live with her. The judge felt that a great ideal and grant her, her request.

Though Jim and his friends were older than I they didn't mine if I hung out with them—in fact they enjoyed my company. We even hung out, sometimes, in nightclubs together; and since I was only seventeen, looking more like fifteen, Jim would give me his [non photo] ID card, date of birth 1939, when I was born in 1943. Moreover, when there was a bouncer-riding shotgun at the bar's door, they'd flatly tell me to get lost.

In addition, I did manage to get into a few bars when there was no bouncer guarding the door. Once inside, Jim and his friends would tease me about my youngness, and how I long to grow up. I knew they were being funny because they also jeered one another. Those were the days of "playing the dozens." Sitting there, in the Golden Nugget nightclub, it the Red Light District with the big boys, drinking my beers, I felt as grown as they did. Hell, I flirted with young women who were no older than I was, and who thought I was cute. Moreover, I watched a myriad of whores sitting at the bar drinking and waiting for tricks to pick them up.

My second year in Boston I stopped hanging with Jim and his contemporaries and took to hanging with a Sugar Hill gang, known as The Lord Sociable. Hence, three months after I joined the gang, our captain, Sweeney, received a serious beating by members of The Ambassadors, a gang from the Grove Hall area, who ambushed him, one night, in a dark alley off Bower Street. The night that happened, The Lord Sociable was at our gang's hangout, at Frank Poolroom, waiting for Sweeney, the gang's captain to, appear.

An hour past, still no Sweeney. Just then, an old friend from the neighborhood with short kinky white hair with one leg slightly longer than the other, and who hung out in the poolroom, limped hurried into the poolroom and on to the back, where The Lord Sociable was hanging out. The old fellow, with the smell of alcohol on his breath, told us that Sweeney just been jumped by the Ambassadors … and taken to Boston City Hospital—now called Boston Medical Center.

Upon hearing the news, and the where about the fight had taken place, we each gave the massager some change so he might buy himself a four-ounce bottle of Robitussin AC cough medicine. Then rushed out the poolroom's front door like a heard of wild prairie Mustangs. As we ran down Humboldt Avenue with our "K55," a five-inch black-handle knife, in our pockets, my heart, boomed in my chest, similar to a jackhammer pounding beams into the ground. I was petrified to what might await us yet, I had the adrenaline pumping for a rumble.

"Look!" Tony whispered pointing to a figure moving toward us, in the semi-dark alley of Bower Place, "someone out there."

We saw it too, and spread out moving toward the figure hoping it would be The Ambassadors. K55, now ready and opened in our hands, we slowly treaded toward the figure when we heard the voice of authority in the night.

"Melvin! If that you, you better get your ass in the house! There been enough trouble here, in this ally tonight!"

The figure and voice was that of Mr. Simpson, Melvin's father, who lived with his family, in one of the three dilapidated houses stilled standing on Bower Place. Similar to his father, Melvin also tall and slander with a honey complexion did not talk back to his father, but walked towards their, on its last legs, apartment building. In addition, the rest of us walked to City Hospital to see about the captain.

There, a young doctor wearing a pair of clogs on his feet and the standard doctor's arteries met us in the corridor. As he spoke to us, he continued, with his right thumb flicking, the top of a ballpoint pen, as if it were a cigarette lighter.

"Your friend," he said, "has gone up to the operating room and may not live through the night."

Since The Ambassadors had attacked the Sweeney, and on our turf, we knew, we had to retaliate on their turf at Grove Hall, which was another part of Roxbury. John L., the gang's lieutenant and next in line to be captain, decided we go home and meet the following evening at the poolroom ready to rumble. There were no drive-by shooting in those days; rumbling was hand-to-hand combat, gladiator fashion!

That evening, after work, I reported to the poolroom where The Lord Sociable had already assembled. Bumpy, one of the gang members, jaundice-colored skin, buckteeth, and body hard as a rock, and Out Law, another gang member, both met me at the door and walked me over to the back of poolroom, where the other four members stood chatting about the condition of the captain.

We quickly discussed our battle plan and exit Frank Poolroom, nonchalance not to draw suspicion. Outdoors, we quickly navigated through the streets, of Roxbury, toward our target; not only did we want to get the fight over with we also wanted to get out of December's foul weather.

Once reaching the square at Grove Hall, we crouched down behind the cars, lining Blue Hill Avenue, across the street from the Grove Hall Bowling Alley. We saw no Ambassadors standing outside the bowling alley, which was their hangout. The weather was foul and much too cold, even for a polar bear.

Just as Frank Poolroom, on sugar hill, was the Lord Sociable turf and hangout, thus, the bowling alley at Grove Hall, was the turf of The Ambassadors. We were neck deep in their territory and in a minute, we'd be in their faces.

Since Melvin, Corbin, and John L. were the biggest and tallest of the group they led the way into the bowling alley. Talking about height, our captain was only 5-2.

John L. tall, lean, and alluring with smooth blue-black skin, and looking like Nat King Cole, peeked into the bowling section and signaled to us by shaking his head from side-to-side, indicating he saw no Ambassadors among the few cheerful bowlers. Down the hall, at the entrance to the poolroom, John L. hastily stopped; backed up, and with his right hand lifted four fingers pointing towards the back of the poolroom.

"Good," I heard myself whispered as we rushed between the pool tables toward the back of the room and surprisingly sprung upon the four Ambassadors, who were playing pool, like lions upon its prey.

A strange yearning came over me. I wanted to fight, to rumble. I wanted to feel the blows on my body, and the clash of body force against body force. This fight would help me get some therapy and get my shit out too. I needed to burn off all the bull dung from the time of Mama leaving, my farm experience, no father, reform school, and the lost of my childhood home.

As we beat down our antagonists with pool-balls, car antennas, and K55s, I felt something cold against my back. I thought it was the cold steel of an Ambassador's knife. However, when I looked behind me there were two mammoth built men, who owned the place, spraying us down with fire extinguishers.

"Get out!" they thundered, as if speaking from one mouth. "You tug from Humboldt think you can come to Grove Hall and mess with me!" Roared, one of the gargantuan spraying the water.

While the other man looking, like Shrek, animated character, continued hosing us and woofed, "Get out of my damn place, you bums!" With that said, they released the triggers of the extinguishers, but kept the hoses pointed at us and yelling, "Get out! Get out!"

Not one of the four Ambassadors had they intentionally spread. Nevertheless, the Ambassadors were bleeding from head and body wounds, for we had pounced upon them out of nowhere making the beat down swift, taking only a few minutes.

"Damn man!" John L. made fun, as we hurried from the poolroom toward the exit.

"Yeah," Out Law roared, as we rushed from the bowling alley into the freezing night. "I know they felt that ass whipping!" We all felt pleased that we had avenged the captain's tragedy and done it without any harm coming to us.

John L., who forever had a smile on his face, no matter what the moment, and who loved joking around, burst out with that unique laugh of his and said, "Man! We were on fire."

"Let's get off this square," I uttered, my teeth chattering, as we ran across the street to the cabstand and poured into the first cab in line. The cabby, a friendly looking white guy with a long white beard, looking like Santa, turned around, looked at us as we piled five-deep onto the back seat, and shook his head from side-to-side, but only asked where we were going.

The gang dropped me off first, leaping from the cab I ran up the stoop two at a time. Inside the warm breezeway, I heard the music of rhythm and blues coming from Mother's apartment and felt safe, and sound again. Before putting my key into the lock, I listened to the chatting going on within and remembered that tonight was Christmas Eve and Mother's party.

Well here I go. I unlocked and opened the door, stepped into the house and closed the door lightly behind me. Dudley, my stepfather Jesse's brother, who already had a few drinks stood in the front corridor, holding a cocktail and, conversing with his tall firm blackberry completion Nigerian fiancée, was the first to notice me. For he faced the door I'd entered.

"Oren!" He exclaimed, then lowered his voice and gave me a Bacchus grin. "Boy, what you're doing all soaked and wet in this kind of weather?"

Rose, his African fiancée, turned looked me up-and-down with large, sexy brown eyes, which caused my sexuality to flicker said, "Oren, please go put on some dry clothes. Do you want to die?"

On my way to my room, I got another question from a foxy young woman whom I knew not standing in the corridor with a young man who said, "Don't tell me it's raining outside?" I just smiled at her and entered my small room.

Dudley knew me well, thus, I knew that he knew that I'd gotten into some shit out there tonight. For he to shot pool at Frank Poolroom and knew that I was involved in one of the sugar hill gangs. Because most of the family and guests were in the living room, dining room and kitchen, only a few guests saw me come in. Outside my room I could hear Mother laughing in the kitchen, while the aroma of her spicy Creole cooking came seeping through my door.

After showering and dressing afresh, I stepped from my room wearing a pair of charcoal-brown slacks, a sunburned colored wool sweater, and on my feet a pair of brown alligator loafers. I went first into the kitchen where I heard the voices of both Jim and Johnny. These guys, when together with Dudley and Daddy Jesse, were funny as hell.

Moreover, the more they drink their Old Grand Dad, White Horse Scotch, and dark Rum, the funnier they became. The nice thing about this working class of men; they were funny when the parties were over, too. I enjoyed being in their company. What is more, my stepfather waited readily to help me any way he could; however, I did not ask anything of him.

This came more from my shyness, than me not liking him—he was a good man.

There in the kitchen, I found Johnny, my sister, Laura's husband, my cousin Jim, Jesse and his brother, Dudley, standing around Mother's kitchen table with drinks in their hands, talking shit. However, they loved sport and enjoyed talking it. Except for Jesse, all these men were playboys and womanizers. They were also good looking men, knew it, and so did the women.

Jim saw me first and didn't hesitate to begin the night by riding me. "Boy, what kind of deep shit you been it tonight," he teased. "We know you came home all wet, looking like a polar bear."

"Hay Jim," Dudley bellowed from where he stood behind the kitchen table near one of the, café curtained windows. "His ass was wet from his neck to his feet. He was so cold that instead of shivering, the boy vibrated. Rose told him to go shower or else he'd vibrate the house away." Everyone, in the kitchen laughed and found Dudley's lie funny.

I thought it funny myself and gave a, "ha, ha."

"Here," Johnny gibed, passing me his glass of whiskey on ice, "take a swig, that'll warm you up."

"Y'all think I'm funny, hmph?"

"Hell yea," Jim said. "You go swimming in sub-zero weather, and you don't think that's funny?" They really got a chuckle from that and, they all began nattering at the same time. "Take a sip," Johnny continued. "You know you want to—"

I took the glass and down the thumb amount of whisky left in, and gave the empty glass back to my brother-in-law. As they were applauding me for downing the whisky without making a face Mother and Laura, entered the kitchen and throw us out.

"Get out, get out my kitchen; vamoose!" Mother played as she shooed us out. "Can't you see I'm cooking?" All the time Mother had been in the dining room setting the table and gossiping with Laura, Rose, and a few guests who had already arrived.

FIVE

HOW I BECAME a JUNKY

The holidays had past and so did the years. It was, November 1966, a dry, chilly, morning; and the sky, similar to my mood was gray when I stepped out of my Vale Street, Roxbury apartment building. I'd been in Boston for some six years, and had been married for three of them. The street gangs were no more and I no longer worked at M.I.T.—in fact, I'd already served six months in the Deer Island House of Correction for car thief. My aim for the day, to hook up with Doug and Conway, buddies of mine who I'd both met at Deer Island a few months ago while serving our sentences.

When I arrived at Conway's' rooming house on Concord Square, in the South End, Doug had already arrived. The two were duo red bones, with light-colored complexions, a shade lighter and they would have been mulattos. They both stood about the same, six feet tall. Doug had terrible feet and walked as though the next step he took would pain his foot. While Conway, who had also come out of New Orleans, but whom had been in Boston for years, spoke colloquial, mixed with an ancestral dialect passed down from his enslave ancestors. Conway spoke so country, that it sounded comical.

Conway answered my knock on his door, and I entered the room to find Doug standing over a small wood table. Conway went back to look over Doug's shoulder making sure that Doug didn't slip him a water shot, instead of the heroin. After emptying two bags of heroin into a wine cap, which addicts called their cooker, Doug poured two eyedroppers of water over the heroin. He then held the very tip of the wine cap between his thumb and index finger, and gently moved it back and forth over a stubby lit candle, sitting on the table.

However, I'd been on the hustling scene for some time, I'd not yet used heroin or even seen it until now. Nevertheless, I knew enough from talk, to know that the cooker contained heroin, cooking in a few drops of water in order to dissolve the white powder. The odor of heroin circling the tiny room both frightened and excited me, causing my *kundilini* to rise to my throat; then, quickly dropped down to my genitals—it felt sinister.

From the small table Doug picked up two makeshift syringes: eyedroppers with hypodermic needle attached to each tips. He drew up the heroin into the syringes, making sure each dropper had equal amounts in them. Doug gave Conway his set of works—the makeshift syringe—and kept the other set of works for himself.

"Let us each put a drop back in the cooker for Elow," Doug suggested. Thus, they ever, so carefully, each left one drop of heroin in the cooker for me, about 2 mg.

Since, I knew nothing about injecting myself with any type of drugs. Doug after getting off in his armpit and then washed out the works in a clean glass of water, which sat on the small wood table drew up the tiny amount of heroin.

"Come on man!" Doug teased. "Come ride the horse."

Heroin was something I'd heard a lot about while I frequent the jails and house of corrections. The incarcerated addicts talked of it, as though it were their, elation.

The addict couldn't wait for his discharge date to appear, to get back out there in the streets, and use heroin toward another addiction, toward another incarceration, or toward his death. I knew all these things; still I stood before, Doug, with my arm stretched out before him waiting to become a junky, waiting to give my life to the street. In the background, with the syringe still stuck into his armpit Conway grunted, "Yeahhh."

"This is it," I said as Doug tied a shoestring around the upper part of my arm. With one of his hands, he slapped a vein near my armpit to inflate in more. Then took the syringe and gently tapped the needle into the vein and, *Tout-de-suite*, I felt what I thought was heaven.

"Damn." I whispered. "This is better than an orgasm." However, with heroin, the orgasm isn't one of sexuality; and yet it's as salacious and demanding as sex.

After my shot, I stood near the made twin bed, narcotized: Eyes nearly closed, knees bent in the dope fiend dip, which resemble the yoga's forward-bend, rocking my body to-and-foe, to the sound of jazz playing on the radio that set on the window-ceil. I kept rocking and humming to the music—higher than high. Moreover, I would not have exchanged my feelings, for the love of Cleopatra. No woman, no matter how princely, could give me the kind of feeling that heroin gave. Heroin became my madam and I her slave. If she said bark, I barked.

"He going' out!" Conway exclaimed. "Oh shit, he O-D-in'!"

"No," Doug replied unperturbed; "he's not over dosing, he's just fucked up. He'll be all right once outside."

I really cannot explain just how two drops of heroin made me feel other than, "satisfying." I found myself in a state of complete will being and very free of all my problems. Taking that first shot, that day, in that small South End rooming house would be my life's biggest mistake, and the beginning of a fiendish, street lifestyle.

Two weeks past with me getting high on heroin on the daily basis; nothing could go wrong I thought, for heroin meet my every need. However, one morning I woke up with a runny nose, cramps in my stomach, pain in my joints, my bowel boiling inside of me like an active volcano; I thought I might be coming down with a serious cold. Tell, I remembered what Doug and other addicts had said to me about the symptoms of being dope sick—and how it felt like the flu.

I rolled out of bed, around noon, and found my wife, Marcia, in the bathroom washing dippers. She took one look at me and asked was I coming down with a cold. "I hope you not coming down with a cold!" she said. "That make me and the children sick. I already got enough work without them getting sick."

Irritable and dope sick I snapped at her, "I don't have a cold, so don't worried!" Marcia, whom I'd met at the movie, in 1961, began dating and before long, in '62 had our first daughter, Theresa. Our son, Darryl, was born a year later, in '63, the year we got married. Shortly after that in '64 Pam was born. Then, in 1966, the same year I was introduction to heroin, our daughter Gwenwtte was born and became our forth and last child.

On Washington Street, a block from our apartment, I flagged a cab and had him drive me in to town, to the Apollo Poolroom on the corner of Columbus and Massachusetts Avenue, in the South End.

In the Apollo Poolroom, which was jammed tight with street people, I walked over to Mack who was already removing a fresh bundle of heroin, wrapped with an elastic band from a hole in the tattered cushioned chair on which he sat. As I mounted the shoeshine stand and took a seat at his side, I sneaked him a ten-dollar bill, and he slid me a bag of heroin. "This real good shit," Mack said, pinching the tip of his nose and showing his sparkling white teeth in a broad smile.

"I hope so," I said scoping the joint filled with tobacco smoke, pool shakes playing high stake pool, pimps talking shit, con men bragging about the money they con out of their last victim, and craps shooters throwing dice across a pool table tuned in to dice table, at the rear of the poolroom.

All drug dealers will boast that their dope is the "best"; and ever buyers hope he's telling the truth. Nevertheless, addicts never know how good the dope is until they shoot it up. With my bag tucked into my watch pocket, I dismounted the shoeshine stand where Mack had just finished getting his lizard skinned, shoes shined.

"I'll be somewhere on the strip if you need me," Mack said, as I exit the Apollo.

Leaving the Apollo, I walked the few blocks up Columbus Avenue to Concord Square, and on to Conway's room, sick and dry heaving all the way.

Over the past two weeks of my addiction, I'd learned how to cook my on heroin and get myself fixed up. Hence, while I got off, Conway already jammed stood in the forward-bend posture, nose almost touching his knees, rocking back-and-forth on his heels listening to a jazz piece. Some junkies once high enjoyed cleaning their place of dwelling from top to bottom. Every high could turn in to an April cleaning for a clean junky. Similar to me, Conway was one of those who enjoyed cleaning when high, and his little spot was spick and span. A fact, addiction caught up to me and turned me into a snake, the lowest of-the-lowly. As the junkies puts it I, had "a monkey on my back." Though, Married I can't say that I felt awful or shamed about being hooked. Rather, I felt that I belong to a certain group of people—the hustling class, the street player—and the sound of jazz.

I'd already established myself as a hustle and a second-story man, or thieve before I'd begun using stuff. Therefore, no matter what state I traveled to, whether New York, Saint Louis, Kansa City, Atlanta ... I got respect from the players in those cities. I wasn't just any player in town; I was a player from, Boston.

In the 1960s, Boston hustlers had a great deal of respect out there on the road when traveling. That's because Boston was dubbed, "Players' Town." Where hustlers came from as far away as Texas and as close as the New York City and Rhode Island to break bread with the Bean Town domestic players, to enjoy Boston's vibrant night life, and to make money which fell from the sky, like rain.

It wasn't until the early 1980s, that the new breed of players and pimps, hustles, addicts, and drug dealers begun looking raunchy; thus, turning Boston's street game in to a new breed of gangs, gang wars, and drive-by shootings. Crack cocaine turning Boston in to the Wild West. Moreover, around that same time, dope dealers from New York had moved in and took over Boston's streets and a few housing developments, and begun dealing both their heroin and crack cocaine out of them.

However, the common people who were trying to raise their children, in these communities and housing developments, had better not oppose the dealer's vigor behavior or snitch to the cops on them, or else. ... For years, the New York boys controlled Boston's dope scene and petrified the community with violence and intimidation.

The two drug lords, who supplied and spread their poison through out Boston urban cities and neighboring towns around it, went by the name of "Foot." Foot was nobody's fool; he had taken his many drug dollars and had invested it in some of New York and New Jersey finest real estate. Moreover, people didn't call him Foot just because his feet were large. He got the street name, "Foot" because he wore on his feet, alligator shoes only.

The other drug lord from New York went by the street name "God." A name given to him by the street kids who he was turning out into the street, to be dope deals and gang bangers. God was so large in the dope world that he opened a large teen community center in Dorchester for the "good kids" where no dope or gang bangers were welcome. Nevertheless, God had really, open the after school program, in order to throw the Boston cops off his trail. In one place he was, so call, helping children in the community with after school activity. A place to meet, play pool games, or ping-pong or chess and even get some GED study. In addition, outside the community center God was training and turning out kids to be gangsters, killers and dope dealers.

However, by the mid 1990s the Boston Police and the Fed did get some control again over the streets of Boston, by placing both Foot and God in federal prison for eons. Nonetheless, by the time this occurred, the New York boys had turned some of Boston's youths into crack fiend, dope dealers and gang bangers. To this day, Boston's inner cities still suffer from the mayhem the New York dope dealers created; then, left behind. They created Boston gangs, as we know it today.

Oh, yes! Heroin at the outset may seem to be just what I needed to control my pains and weaknesses, fears and life's obstacles. Heroin seemed to be the only factor in my life, which cured all my maladies. However, like most gratification it soon wears out.

It wears out when everyday becomes a struggle, and everything in life sinks into the abyss. Providing for family becomes a strain, holding down a job and being honest become impossible, getting up in the morning dope sick and having to pilfer takes a toil. Being addicted to heroin like being stuck in mud up to your neck, you want to get out; however, there is no how, in sight.

Heroin addiction is a corruption, a corruption, which corrupts the addict's mind and will, and will not terminate until it either kills the addict or robs him of self-assurance. To avoid death, prison, and lasting shame; the addict must modify his fiendish behavior, change his ways, and most of all change his life—he must once and for all—slay the horse. Then, and only then will he be free and dignified.

I'd tried many times through "robust therapeutic" drug programs to dig myself free from my addicted behavior. However, I just could not get a grip on it. For heroin was the only voice I heard. Being a junky and criminal meant that I'd done a great deal of time in prison. On the street for no longer than eighteen months, that's if I'm lucky. Then, I'd find myself back in prison for four or five years at a time, leaving my young wife and children in dismay.

Like the night when the household was asleep, two cops came by the house and arrested me on a bench warrant for not appearing in court on the day I was supposing to, and took me to the police station. I'd been out on bail, and on the run for some six months, for breaking and entrancing a house in the daytime to committee a felony.

"Elow," Marcia said undertone, as one of the cops handcuffed me behind my back. "What they doing here—?"

"Oh! Just an old bench warrant," uttered the other cop taking a stalwart hold of my upper arm and usher me toward the door.

"Is he coming back?"

"Nothing to worry about, Miss. Sure he'll be back," the cop holding on to my upper arm assured her, as if he were the judge.

I knew he'd said that to ease the pain he saw in my wife's eyes. Yet I knew better, I knew I was going to prison. That's why I hadn't gone back to court. The kids sleep well during that night and never heard a thing.

An educated guess told me that these two, red face cops were perhaps driving a paddy wagon. For their uniforms were soiled and their black neckties and the front of their shirts, down to their laps were stained with spilled food; their faces were pallid, and a couple their lower shirts buttons had popped off because of their beer-inflated bellies. However, to my surprise, the two chimneysweepers, looking cops, were driving a high polished Boston Police cruiser.

The following morning, I was taken from District "4" Police Station, where I'd spent the rest of the night, by two cops who placed me in the back of a paddy-wagon with five other sad sacks that smelled of jail and took us to Boston Municipal Court. The bench judge, that morning was Judge Attlow, short, bald and punchy. When I entered the courtroom's holding dock from the holding cell, Judge Attlow stood behind his bench. He much preferred standing and moving about his small area, looking like a pool ball, than sit in his tall impressive brown leather chair.

After hearing my case, the judge looked at me over his bifocal and said, "Mr. Elow! This is your, lucky day where you don't go to jail. The good nun whose house you broke into asked that the court not to send you away, to give you another chance. The nun with kind blue eyes was in the courtroom, sitting in the first row, looking with concern directly at me. As soon as my eyes caught hers, I quickly dropped my head and felt like dung. I wished that I could disappear, or swallow my head into my chest.

"I'm going to place you on two years probation and demand you get yourself into a drug program. Your probation officer will help you if you work with him. Do you understand me?"

"Yes your Honor," I replied from the holding dock, as I tried checking my joy of being set free. When I reported to my probation office before leaving the courthouse, the nun was sitting on the oak bench near his office. As I sat at the other end of the bench, she asked how I felt. I told her I felt well and thanked her for not pressing charges. The nun asked if I was Catholic, I told her that I was. We spoke for a few moments about my addiction and my getting into NA. She reminded me of my eight-grade nun, Sister Jones Maria who taught me at Saint Paul Catholic School in my youth. They both had a deep love for souls in pain.

It was ten pass eleven by the time I walked out into the fresh morning air. I wasn't yet dope sick; nevertheless, I could feel it coming on. Just before gone to bed, I'd shot a good bag of heroin, I'd purchased from a dealer named Slick.

I hopped on a Tremont Street bus at Park Street Station and hopped off at Concord Square, between West Newton Street and Massachusetts Avenue. Just as I'd imagine, there on the corner of Concord Square and Tremont Street, underneath the "Big Tree" I found Slick, with his rotten flesh and infective body of abscess, standing in a group with other lawless buddies, discussing the first wave of Caucasians moving into the South End.

"White people gone take the South End over and take it to another dimension," Slick said as I stepped among the group. "I'm serious, you just wait." When he notice my head signal, to come over, he stepped away from the boys, into a nearby doorway.

"One," I said.

"The dope good," he said looking at me; "no, I'm serious. This the real shit!"

"Yeah, baby," I said, "I know, I bought two bags from you last night."

"Yeah, yeah, then you know this's real shit!"

This dude was short and ugly, five feet five with that dirty, yellow looking skin. I moved in on his excitement and asked for a bag on the cuff. To my surprise, he pulled another bag from the bundle in his hand and gave it to me. "I want my money tomorrow!"

Slick was a pig when it came to using both heroin and cocaine, and a pit bull when it came to mood swings. He was the kind of fiend that sat in front of the cooker for hours shooting up piles of heroin mixed with cocaine. Because he had used up his veins, he'd shoot his dope into his abscesses, into veins in his private part, his neck, and other part of his body. By the time, he'd finished shooting up, his arms and legs … were a bloody mess from trying to find a vein; thus causing his body to form more sores, which left him smelling like the Boston City Mouge.

One late evening, when Massachusetts and Columbus Avenue were booming with people out having a good time, a shotgun blast sounded in the night coming from the direction of St. Botolph Street. It seemed as tough the news coming from the hustler's grapevine hit the streets before the shotgun smoke had cleared the air, "Slick just got shot and his guts all over the stoops on St. Botolph Street!"

With the two bags, I headed over to Conway's rooming house. Conway, who was in a node down to his knees escalated from thus position and went over to the wood table where he removed, from one of the small drawers, a tan, suede leather pouch and passed it to me. I removed the works from it; I then, connected the needle to the eyedropper and from a glass of water, Conway had on the table, I half filled the makeshift syringe with the water, cooked the heroin in the wine cap, and got off on one of the bags. After shooting up, I gave Conway two dollars for the use of his place and works.

When leaving Conway's, I got on the Tremont bus and went straight home to 51 Vale Street, where the Elow family presided. When I entered the apartment of four bedrooms, Marcia was in the front room with a dust-cloth in one hand a can of furniture spray in the other dusting furniture. As soon as we laid eyes on each other, we rush into each other arms. With her arms around my neck and my hands cupping her tight little butt, we kissed deeply, while trying to squeeze our bodies into one.

"Elow!" Marcia roared, as she backed away. "You smell like funk from being in jail!"

"Oh, you know you like it."

"No, nothing until you shower!" Still I went after her; I was on a sexual roll and wanted more than kisses. However, with pettiness and swiftness on her side she got by me and, dashed toward the kitchen. Thus, I turned and went into the bathroom.

As I showered the aroma of frying bacon seep its way into the bedroom, through hot steam and vapor and found its way to my nostril. By the time

I'd finished in the bathroom, Marcia was calling me to eat. Though past two o'clock in the afternoon, my wife knew what would make me happy after spending a night in jail, cooked my favorite country-style breakfasts: Two sunny-side-up eggs perfectly cooked, where the yokes stared up at me, and the white cooked through. Moreover, there was crisp fried bacon, home fries smothered in onion, buttered toasts and jelly, and a tall glass of cold milk. Before eating, though, I took a few tokes of Columbian gold and then place the joint back in the ashtray.

The next morning I got dressed, stuck my screwdriver into the sleeve of my full-length leather coat, and without saying a word to anyone, not even kids who were playing in the bedroom near the kitchen. Outside the snow had begun falling and sticking to the frigid ground, giving the city the feel of Christmas, which was only two weeks away.

I made my way down Marcella Street, passing Marcella Park, and on to Jackson Square, to the bus stop on Columbus Avenue. When the bus pulled up, I got on and asked the driver for a free ride. The man looked me up and down, with a smile cracked across his face and asked me, why should he.

I looked at the old, timeless bus driver who were looking at retirement, with his uniform cap tipped lightly to right of his head, smile and said, "Come on it's Christmas. I'll pay you this fare next time—I'm only going to Mass Ave."

"Yeah, yeah," the driver mimic, sure you'll pay next time."

"I well."

"Go ahead, only because it's Christmas."

I got off the bus at Massachusetts Avenue and Tremont Street, walked down Tremont, pasting Crowley's fry chicken joint, which smelt like chicken, fired in burnt cooking oil. At the Big Tree, where addicts and drug dealers hung out under, I crossed Concord Square and entered Lucky Lounge. There in the semi-darkness I noticed a couple dealers standing together with their backs against the wall and their eyes on the door watching for both cops and clients.

When I approached the two, they both whispered, as if they were mockingbirds "I got it."

"I got the real shit, though," said the other pusher.

I spoke to one then the other about me being dope sick and my being broke; however, neither would cuff me. No! Was a typical answerer that dealers gave; they got off by listening to a sick addict ask them for a cuff. That's one of the reasons I'd robbed them every good chance I got. I left the lounge feeling less than a man both for being an addict and for bowing down to two greasy headed dealers.

If an addict got himself hooked, he'll do just about anything for a shot of heroin. When he's sick and has no money or nothing to turn it to quick cash, he's at his weakest human point. At that point, most, if not all, would steal from their mother or other family members, or anyone else. I'd steal from anyone for a fix, none excluded.

Yes, asking dealers for a cuff hurt; however, junkies are full of psychological agony where many other things in their lives hurt, them. That's what they're running from; they're running from a group of horrifying feelings, feelings which they believe can only be rid of by doping their agony with dope. They don't let their shame over rule their addiction, for if shame stood in their pathway there'd be no addiction.

When a junky is dope sick, his body on pins and needles, his nerves system agitated; when he's vomiting up yellowish green bile and his bowler wants to let go; when every muscle hurt and the hair on his arms seemed to turn back into the skin and grind against the internal raw flesh, would do about anything. Moreover, when compulsion driven anxiety takes over, he may even do heartless things, trying to get money to get straight.

Outside the win had picked up making the weather seems a lot colder than it actually was. I stop and button my leather coat to its neck and begun canvassing an area for about an hour, before coming upon an apartment building, I found simple to enter. Thus, I walked up the stoops, pushed open the front door and entered the breezeway. For a second or two while holding my breath, I listened for voices or sound, all was quite. I checked the door that led into the apartment complex; this one was locked, not a problem, though, for locks, are made for honest people.

I removed the screwdriver from my coat sleeve and in a zippy popped the lock. I stepped into the hallway that smelt of Christmas pine wreaths, which hung from the apartment doors. Again, I held my breath and listened; and only quietness filled my ears. Hence, I decide to work the first floor, and moved liked a cat toward apartment "One" and gently knocked on the door, no answer.

In a snap, I opened door and fleetly closed and locked it behind me. I listened; then, ran through the house, on tiptoes, to the kitchen looking for an escape route in case someone tried entering the front door. Good! There was a back door, which led to an alley and out to the street. Moreover, the apartment was foundry hot.

Near the window in the living room was a large heavenly decorated Christmas tree where the tip of the angel's crown nearly touched the motif Victorian ceiling. Moreover, just like that, lying there on the coffee table among books and periodicals was a wad of cash, which really got my heart pounding. Without bothering how much money I had, I slipped the money into my pocket and went through the rest of the things sitting on the table. I then made my way into the only bedroom and removed the hand full of gold and men jewelry from the dresser's top and drawers. It took me no more than six minutes to search the small apartment. On my way out the comfortable apartment, I removed a shoulder bag, which contained a Nikon camera, and lenses from a coat rack near the front door and throw it over my left shoulder.

Outside, I trembled from head to feets, not from the frosty weather but from the idea that I'd soon have a fix. Just the thought of heroin in my veins and the silkiness it brought to my body and mind intensified my anxiety to where I began vomiting again. Heroin had a chokehold on my life, and its mission—to drag me through the larva of my own destruction. However, before my destruction I must first dig my own grave. A grave that thousands of other heroin addicts had dug before me, because the deeper I dug the more bones I shoveled up.

My nerves now completely agitated and the few blocks walk to the Rainbow Lounge at Tremont and Springfield Street seemed endless. In the lounge, lit with soft red light, I made my way through the buzzing of voices, a thick crowd of good timers and cigarettes smoke, to the back and ran in to one of the same dues who'd refused me a cuff, earlier at Lucky. I looked around to make sure no one were eyeballing us and removed the entire bank-roll from my pocket, peeled off a hundred-dollar bill and slipped it to the dealer. "Give me ten," I whispered dictatorially.

"Damn Elow?" he thought, "an hour ago you asking for a bag on the cuff, now you're rich." The dealer stuck his fingers underneath his thick slimy Jheri curls, hairstyle, and pulled a small aluminum foil package from it and passed it to me. "There's ten in there."

"Hay Elow!" the parasite dealer declared. "You know all that money you got belong to us dope dealers."

"Yeah and Santa Claus, Too, I replied as I eased through the crowd and out the door.

That day I didn't go over to Conway's room; instead I crept into a second floor bathroom in one of the many rooming houses. Once in the bathroom, off the hallway, I pulled my works from my nylon sock where I usually kept them when I was in the street, and placed them on top of the sink. I tore a couple bags opened and poured the white powder into the cooker. From the sink, I pulled up a few drops of water into the makeshift syringe—squeezed the water over the heroin lit two matches together, and slowly cooked the dope until it had dissolved. I tied my upper left arm with my belt, found a vein near its pit, and pushed the solution into it. Therefore, as quick as lighting I felt my body spring into life. Feeling triumphant I short of giggled, "He's alive, he's alive!"

SIX

THE BLIND LEADING the BLIND

W hen I got home, Marcia was in the bathroom washing linen diapers in the bathtub. With four children, she kept busy around the house; then, she worried about me as well. Marcia was used to keeping house she often babysat, washed, cleaned, and cooked for her five siblings, slightly under her age, while her parents worked.

"Elow!" You goanna die one of these days from pneumonia walking around your chest all out in this kind of weather" Marcia billowed. "Don't coming running to me when you get sick."

What sick, I thought. When the addict has had his antifreeze, or his heroin, coldness and foul weather meant little to him. The Addict, soullessly, live a strange life, he's under the impression that heroin is his complete problem solver for all that ails him. Therefore, being dope sick, committing crime, losing family and love ones, going to prison, and even death are worth the high—the hooks and the crooks of the game. All his being, good and bad is, wrapped up in the authority of the "bag," the white horse running wild.

"I'm Okay," I said pulling Marcia's body against mines. We were young and made love like rabbits; and we enjoyed each other bodies, as well. Thus, most times when I came home, I'd go right up to my wife and tried sexing it up.

"Elow," she'd laughed; then, wiggled her foxy little body away, "I'm trying to do my work."

46

"Oh come here," I'd played, "you know you like it."

"Not now, honey, I got too much to do right now." Marcia knew I had a habit and had seen me, only once, injecting myself, in the twenty-two years we had been married.

Marcia was charming, clean, soft spoken, and a supper mom and wife. She was all a man need in a woman, and I loved her deeply. However, how does a junky explain his love when his life and his mentality are slaves to his mistress, heroin. Yet, our love prevailed for many years, before I ferociously ran my family off with my love for heroin and the street. Moreover, the shame is, after all those years, I divorced her for a junky stripper, my life's greatest mistake.

The next afternoon Marcia took of the money I'd given her and went Christmas shopping, while I stayed home with the kids: Teresa then five-years-old and Darryl four, Pam three and Gwenie, one. I was a much better father when high. In fact, I didn't feel at all comfortable around my children unless high. I felt unworthy of their love. Nevertheless, whenever I could make it up to them, there weren't a better father and husband than me. On the other hand, however, when I was dope sick I'd turn into a maniac, a Doctor Jekyll and Mr. Hyde. I would scream at my daughters, flogged my son and insulted my wife. As much as I was a junky, I was utterly demented.

Nonetheless, I did not tolerate, at all, my children not doing well in school or acting out in public. Nor did I allow them to talk back to their mother or me; I also didn't want my children going through life untutored thus, I constantly preached education and more education to them. Most of the time when I was not incarcerated, I really tried making sure that my family was taking care of; nevertheless, I had failed fatherhood and marriage, big time. Heroin demanded every minute in my life and became my boss, my lover, and my Satan.

Ever Christmas and New Year, we'd invite family and friends over to our Holidays dinners, where we enjoyed the joy of life. Marcia cooked both Christmas and New Year dinners and made the cakes and pies, too. The children were radiant with gladness, while Marcia played host to the guests, drink her twelve-year old Scotch, chased with beer, and had a ball, while listening to R&B.

Well, anyway, a few mornings after New Year I woke up broke and dope sick, heroin had waken me with a running nose, hot and cold flashes, muscle-aches, body-spasms, and unsettling-nerves. Yet I remained in bed wiggling around like a snake on fire. Finally, heroin pulled me out of bed, and kicked me out of my comfortable and warm apartment onto the frigid street, as if I were his dirty whore.

Now up and dope sick, broke, and in my Doctor Hyde's mood, I look to carry out my lush with heroin and would not stop or go home again until my wishes, to getting high, was completed. Marcia, who had learned to recognize my ugly characteristics, said nothing to me. Now that I look back on those dreadful days, I can see just how confusing her young mind must have been of my behavior, a loving human being one moment and a complete psychopath the next. That monstrous behavior of mine also had the children on edge all the times. Nevertheless, not that deep down inside of me, though, was a loving person who wanted to be a first-rate husband to my wife and a father to my kid. Marcia was a darling who never gave up on me.

Never, I gave up on her.

Walking out the apartment front door I could hear, in my head, the voice of bubble-eyed, the Jheri curled, dope dealing maggot from the Rainbow whispering in my ear, *I told you all that money you was flashing before Christmas, was the dope man's money.* He was partially right though. However, most of the cash and gold I'd turned into cash went to buy the children Christmas offerings and to celebrate both Christmas and New Year dinners. In addition, I had made enough money to keep myself out of the street for some ten days and had a merry, Merry Christmas and a Happy New Year. I often made good money in my crime of choice. My BMW was bought and paid for with money I'd stolen from breaking into people's homes.

That was ten days I didn't have to worry about getting buster and going to prison, nor did I have to worry about being dope sick. For ten days, we were just one big happy family. Though sick, it pleased me to see the powdery snow rapidly falling to the ground outside. Snow, rain, and bad weather were an optimal time for me. If the weather was gray and wet, and ugly, then most likely people are in a gray mood, as well, and not very observant, or looking out of their windows.

I canvas the streets for what seemed like eternity before I found a building that looked rich and free of its occupants. I climbed the stoops, rang the doorbell a few times. When no one answered, I looked behind me into the street and saw two young males—head down, slogging through snow, on the un-shoveled sidewalk, toward me. One of them held a large red white and blue colored umbrella over both their heads; and passed by without, so much as lifting their heads.

I pulled the screwdriver from the sleeve of my black wool topcoat, quickly stuck the point between the door and doorframe, near the lock, and popped it opened.

Just as I entered the apartment, I notice an elongated medal with a round hole in its center pointing in my direction; and as quickly as I'd noticed the medal, I noticed the whole scene and froze. There, sitting on the stairs that led to the floors above was a man, in his early thirties wearing an Angela Davis look-a-like afro, pointing a single barrel shotgun at my face. He was quite calm, yet, full of authority when he spoke, looking me in the eyes.

"I've been watching you," he said, the gun still leveled at my face. "I even heard and saw you, when you tried breaking into my back door. But you couldn't get in—"

"I didn't know you were home," I meekly said, making sure only my lips moved. My body remained fixed staring at the gun and listening to the voice pointing it.

"Does that make it right to break into my house or anyone else place, if they're not home?" he said raising his voice, but never taking the gun off me.

"I'm sorry, man," I pleaded, putting on my baby-face. For now, I felt that if he intended to shoot me, he would have done so by now. Nevertheless, he could call the cops.

"I only do this because I'm strung out on heroin," I rapped. "If it wasn't for heroin, I wouldn't be breaking into people's homes."

"You got a habit, huh?" he said resting the gun across his lap. With the gun remove to his lap, my entire body, and even the apartment itself seemed to relax. Today wasn't my death day. Before I knew what he would do, next I begged him not to call the cops. I told him that I had a wife and four children to care for and didn't want to go to jail and leave them alone. He asked had I ever sort help for my problem.

"No." I implied apprehensively.

"Tell you what; if you agree to let me take you to this inpatient drug program, off Tremont Street, where a friend of minds is its director, I want shoot you or call the cops." Quite naturally, I agreed.

When the towering body-toned young man stood up and walked over to a hallway closet underneath the stairs he'd dismounted, I noticed just how tall and Spartan his built. He carefully broke the shotgun down, removed the shell and slung the shotgun shut—"click." He then, placed the gun in the far left side corner of the closet.

From the closet, he removed a black leather jacket and put it on over a heavy white captain sweater. From the pockets of his coat, he pulled free both his black beret and thickly lined leather gloves. He then, pulled his beret over half his head and styled it to the right, just below his yellow ear, which went with his yellow complexion.

On his way out the door, the brother a member, of the Black Panther Party, looked at me and calmly said, "Don't leave—use up the program to help you. Your family needs you and you need yourself"

I had not been at the program five hours when I noticed an opening to make my get-a-away, without anyone noticing. It was around 9:00 p.m., and a couple staff members and patients had gathered in the, large, warm family living room, where a small flickering fire burned in the fireplace, to watch television. I nonchalantly, after getting 60 mg. of methadone from the program's nurse walked out the back door. The weather was offensive. The wind wowing northeast and huge flaks of snow, caked over my shoulders as it felled.

On my way home, I walked blocks, in the street, where one or two cars passed me by, once and a while. Down Tremont Street I slogged, moving to one side of the street, to let one of the snow ploughs get by while the howling wind, literary pushing me down the street; and into Lucky Lounge. The bar near empty and the only dealer in the place were bubble eyes, sitting at the bar between two prostitute, looking like an orangutan dressed in an auburn color suit, with rhinestones covering the two large elephant-flapped lapels.

With limited junky pride, I approached the Jhri curled clown and asked for a cuff. "Hay man;" I asked feeling like a worm and lest than the man I was, "man, give me one of them things until tomorrow." The two hookers whom I knew and who had recently begun prostituting and using drug had once both put on a uncanny show for my buddy and me when they first came out in to the street, fresh and naïve.

I had going out to buy a few bags of heroin for me and a friend of mind, when I met the two underneath the Big Tree. They had just bought their dope, and need a place to shoot up. I invited them to come with me; and took them over my friend's room on West Concord Street, where we shot up our dope; then, the uncanny show began.

Not that I needed bubble eyes to cuff me, since I was already stone; off of 60 mg. of methadone. However, a junky can never have enough dope; he's likes a pig that cannot get full, no matter how much he chows.

"What happened to all that cash you was flashing the other day, huhhh?" He asked with a colossal sneer on his greasy face. "I told you it was the dope man's money."

"Come on brother, you know I'm good for it."

"I'm your brother now, huh."

"Don't give him shit!" The hooker with the black-chocolate skin exclaimed. "Last summer he took both our money, and throw us out of his buddy's room, after her and I had put a twosome show on for them."

"I done told y'all before, you need a good pimp like me to watch y'all back," bubble said.

"We don't need a pimp!" the little, bit tee white hooker wearing a Peter Pan's hair cut, said snapping, at bubbled eyes.

"That's okay with me—you girls goanna get tired of them junkies' f... with y'all, one day.

To my surprise bubble eyes turned his attention back to me and said, "When you gon pay me if I cuff you a bag?"

"Tomorrow afternoon—"

"Don't f... me around, now," he said, motioning the black chocolate hooker to serve me. She pulled a bag of heroin from the bundle of 20 bags she held in her hand, tied with a rubber band, and passed it to me below the bar.

"Oh, come on baby," I said, "You know you're not mad with me."

I thought of saving the bag for the next day; however, I walked over to Conway's where we both shot up the cuffed bag. Since the drug program had called my wife, during the day, to inform her of my whereabouts, I spent the night at Conway's where we talk about the old western books we'd both read and listen to jazz all night long. The next day I went home, and when Marcia saw me walked into the front door she looked at me and said, "Elow, you not giving, yourself a chance!"

In the spring of 1967, when arrested for breaking into a house, in the daytime to commit a felony, Judge Mike McKinney sentenced me, out of his Roxbury District Court, to an indefinite term at Concord Reformatory. I had out grown jails and house of corrections.

Concord Reformatory was a reformatory only in name, for it was a major medium prison with thirty-foot walls and armed guardhouses. The prison housed some of Massachusetts most brutal convicts. On sentencing me, Judge McKinney also stated that he didn't think Concord would change my behavior, because I was a "junky," and once a 'junky' always a junky." Even then I didn't believe that "always a junk" rhetoric. The judge certainly should have known the status of the junky. For years, the word on the grape vine was that the judge had been snorting cocaine. Moreover, later McKinney made an open statement that snorting coke was "good for you and the law should legalize it."

I spent my first thirty days in Concord on the "new line," the probation blocks, for new inmates. However, I spent that time kicking my heroin addiction. Concord, like Deer Island made the addict kick, cold turkey. Nevertheless, by the time I hit general population I was fine and full of twenty-seven year old energy.

Once in population, I ran into many guys whom I knew from the street and who highly respected me for my street science and fine clothes. Yet the prisoners who intrigued me the most were the ones who wore black baseball caps; they called themselves, "biggies." In other word, they were the prison's convicts who ran the joint and who had ties to the mob. They were the prison: loan sharks, drug dealers, and bookies; taking bets on horseracing, baseball and football. As well, they held the best jobs in the prison and prided themselves on being convicts, and not inmates. The first horse—Danny Boy—I ever betted on was in Concord. The horse won and paid two to one and my two packs of cigarettes, betted, brought me four packs.

Latter on, in my sentence I became all right with the whole lot of biggies; all right enough for them to trust me and to pull me out of that filthy dusty cement shop where, I worked making concert, sewage, pipes for the city of Boston.

Doc Savage, a slender pale face convict who wore a toupee under his black cap, transferred me from the cement shop, where I'd been working, to the prison's mess hall—one of the best jobs in the prison. That wasn't and easy job to get, especially, if African American and people of colors. Someone had to vouch for such a high quality job. For the mess hall crew and the kitchen crew ate well and had the privileges of going out into the "big yard" during work hours. While other prisoners worked, either in the laundry room, print shop, school building; in the cement shop, and boiler room … The mess hall crew and the kitchen crew, along with the big yard workers rather managed both the big yard and the main prison.

Doc worked in the job assignment office, so it was quite easy for him to place persons whom he liked in the best jobs. In the evening Doc worked at his trade, as the prison's watch smith repairing watches for both prisoners and guards. Nevertheless, there was a storm side to him as well. Prisoners who knew him whispered that Doc could change from a person into a savage defiant.

Once when Doc and I were serving a few days in isolation for breaking prison rules, he told me why the system transferred him from maximum Walpole State Prison, to Concord Reformatory. Doc said that he and four other convicts had been involved in trying to taking over Walpole, in the 1960s. They had taken the Catholic priest and a prison guard hostage. He spoke of having poured gasoline all over the priest and threatened to touch him. Doc went on that the other prisoners hung the frighten, wet my pants, prison guard—on a hook in the kitchen's meat freezer; then, threatened to let him freeze to death if the administration fails to grant their grievances.

I remember cutting the storyteller off, as he told his narration, and asking him what happen to the hostages. I'd became anxious and wanted him to get finish with the story. I wanted to know, the rest of, what happened.

Doc stretched his arms out his cell, through the bars, gesturing me to look around at the interior of the hole's architectural design: with its steel, gray, stairs and gray steel tiers climbing five stories high and said, "This is where it got me, fifteen-years added to my already life sentence."

I did not wanting to upset him, but I had to know what happen in the takeover. "No, what I mean is what happened to the priest and guard?" I took quite a chance asking him questions in the first place. However, he and I were the only two prisoners in that area of the hole that day—the guards were out of the way sitting at their desks in conversation. Moreover, Doc was in a talking mood so I quiz him, but only about the takeover.

"Nothing happened to the priest," Doc said, "but he did get a buzz snorting up all that gasoline. No, no, I'm just playing." We both laughed. "The guard was a bit blue when we let him go; however, he was back at work the next day."

"How long did y'all hold them hostage?"

"Eight, or nine hours."

"Damn! And he didn't freeze to death?"

"We took him out once and a while."

"Did you get what you wanted?"

"No, we were overcome with teargas, beaten bloody, and dragged away, by C. Os., correctional officers, to spend two years in the underground, "the dungeon," at Bridgewater State Prison, a prison that had been built for confederate war prisoners. Doc said no more; he turned to his bunk and rested. I dear not ask him what were their grievances.

While at Concord, I ran in to some prisoners who were devout readers, who introduced me to fictions and non-fictions, as well as classical: Henry David Theroux, Henry Van Dyke, Walt Whitman, Nathanial Horton, and many other fine books. However, Concord did have a tiny library with an interesting selection of books. Like the old saying goes, "Books are like friends, they should be few and well chosen."

The reason for Concord prison having an interesting collection of books had to do with the nice residents of the towns of Concord and nearby Lexington, who had donated most of the book at Concord library. Not only did the town people donate books, but also they often came inside the wall to give support to the prisoners. In fact, the first paycheck I'd received for my writings came from a sermon I'd written for a Protestant pastor who served one of the churches in the town of Concord. That was 1967, the year my appetite to write begun.

I read many books, on the prison library shelves; however, it was the work and prose of Khalil Gibran that caught my eyes. His writer's voice certainly was that of a sage. I liked Socrates too, "Now I must go, I'm to die and you to live, which is better is known to the gods alone."

Concord would not be the last institution I'd do a great deal of reading in.

A few years early, while doing time at Deer Island House of Correction, before my sentence to Concord Reformatory, I'd met A. C. Hillman, a hustler from Boston, who became my mentor, big brother and friend. A. C. was truly the first person who, help move my interest in the direction of reading, for he read everything. So, by the time I got to Concord I was already a frequent reader. When I met A. C., he was reading Harold Robinson's books, which was, then, popular in the '60s. He also introduced me to the remarkable music of jazz.

Nevertheless, most of the books which I've read, I did so hoping to find, Self and peace of mind, within the pages; for I had no idea what I wanted out of life, and nor did I know my direction. Thus, caught between innocence and crime, I choose crime.

SEVEN

CRIME and PUNISHMENT

After serving a year at Concord, the system released me on parole; and on the morning of my discharged, the administration gave me one of those, heavy wool, charcoal-gray pin-stripe suits and fifty dollars. A glee correctional officer, or CO, in his mid fifty, who occasionally hummed ballads, drove me a short distant from the prison, to the train station at Concord Square. Hence, when the Commuter Rail train arrived he escorted me aboard, and whispered something into the conductor's ear; then, wishing me luck, he turned and stepped off the train humming one of his ballads. The conductor, who was bright and full of life, with his conductor's cap push above his forehead, greeted me as he did all other passengers with a smile and a good morning while, collecting my fair.

I had a new address to go home to, for my wife and children had moved out of Roxbury, and into the Jamaica Plain Housing Project. When I got off the communal Rail train at North Station, I took the old elevated Orange line, the "T," pasting Downtown Boston. Now called, "Down Town Crossing," and exit through the subway tunnel, into daylight at China Town near, the South End. The train past the Holy Cross Cathedral while wobbling on the rails, toward "Forest Hills "T" station, the train's destination.

From the train's windows, I could see much of the city below and the very sight of it literally made me, psychologically, dope sick with chills and hot flashes and all the other bad feelings. Thus, I got off the train at North

Hampton "T" station and walked over to Mack's shooting gallery at West Newton and Saint Botolph Street. In those days ninety, nine percent of the heroin dealing done in greater Boston, took place in the South End.

During the 1960s when the white homosexuals and white settlers begun moving into the South End neighborhood. They found it promising, in spite of the heroin sold from Dartmouth Street to Columbus Avenue, from Tremont to Massachusetts Avenue, and around the block on both Washington and Springfield Street.

Day and night prostitutes tramped up-and-down Mass and Columbus Avenues to Huntington Avenue. While muggers and junkies moved from shadow to shadow in wait of a victim, to rip off. The South End was a little like "Old Forty Second Street" in New York City before Mayor Giuliani cleaned it up.

Anyway, when arriving at the shooting gallery I climbed to the third floor and gently knocked on one of the chipped, smudged and gray painted doors. A few second or so past before a voice inside faintly said, "Hello."

"Elow," I whispered and all of a sudden, I heard bolts, padlock, and deadlocks clicking backward.

Elow, Elow my man," Mack uttered; voice filled with subdued ado flung opened the door and gave me one of those big bear hugs that almost left me feet off the floor. "Man it's good to see you, Elow. Come in; come in, before I draw heat on my crib, his one bedroom apartment. When you get out?" he inquired locking all locks on the door behind us.

"Today," I answered as I followed him into the kitchen, where two slick junkies sat at a round wooden rustic table getting off, which I didn't know, both with syringes in their armpit.

"How many?"

"One."

"Dope's dynamite," Mack warned passing me a small glassine bag while soothingly removing the ten-dollar bill from between my fingers. "If you goanna get off here you know that's two-dollars more."

I cooked the dope and drew it up into an eyedropper Mack had placed on the table beside me. I booted the dope, back and forth, watching the blood flow in-and-out of the syringe, into my arm; then, that was the last thing I remembered until coming to with Mack pressing a towel fill with ice on the back of my neck.

"Man! I thought you a-goanna," Mack uttered, mopping the sweat from his blackberry colored, complexioned, face with his hand. He then, adjusted his hair with a pick-comb, which he kept, wedged into his large afro.

"I tell you, I did everything to bring you out of the OD;" Mack said—from slapping the shit out of you, to walking you back and forth, to pouring ice down your pants. Still you wouldn't come to; then, I remembered the cold wet towel trick and here you are. Boy, you lucky." he said, while pouring two bags of heroin into the cooker for himself.

"Thanks man. You save my life," I said nodding down to my crouch. "I'll never forget you for that."

"Come on, Elow, man, we go way back together. Plus I know you do it for me, if it was me overdosing; man, come on now," Mack grunted as the heroin, in no more a second, flowed from his brain to his nasal, into his throat—where it wraps around his vocal cord causing him to speak through his nose until the dope brought euphoria to his entire body. "Man! The dope is funky," he uttered letting go of the syringe still stuck in his armpit, and began signing, "The dope is funky, the dope is funky, just ask Elow—"

"You're right," I said rubbing my face up-and-down with the palm of my hand.

Mack stopped singing, stood up from the table, where the two junkies still sat, pulled the works out of his armpit and exclaimed, "You two junkies get the f... out my crib! You suckers just sat their like New York junkies looking crazy while he is overdosing. Get the hell out!"

"Man, shit, I don't even know the dude!" impulsively said the junky dressed in a dark green silk shirt, brown slacks, and spotting his hair in finger waves.

"F... that!" said the other dude, wearing gray slacks, a black sweater, and a dark gray beaver hat on his. "I ain't goanna blow my high helping nobody come out of no OD. Come on, Lucky, let's go, man."

"Let's buy our dope now, for later," Lucky said. "Hay, Mack, let me get two."

"Me too, lucky said, "give me Two."

"Yeah, the shit is good and funky, you got to be real careful," Mack uttered, giving the two dudes their two bags apiece.

When the two dudes had left Mack who looked higher than Mount Everest said, "Man, you can tell them bums ain't from Boston."

"Where're they from? I never saw them before."

"Mid west somewhere like that Mack said, as he walked me down the stairs to the front door, teasing me all the way down about my OD.

"You're a funny dude, Man," I laughed and thanked him again for saving my life. Junkies were that way they could look death in the eyeballs, and a few minutes later laughing at it.

I didn't last long out there, on parole, before I was back in Concord. However, while there this time, I got involved in a therapeutic drug program that was being set-up inside the wall for heroin addicts who had now begun crowding up both the prisons and jails system. The time was late spring, the beginning 1970.

I was truly, fed up with being an addict, moreover, I knew that if I broke free from heroin that had taken control of my body and mind, I'd be a much better man. Heroin had already taken my life and turned me in to a person without feelings for others. That wasn't my Catholic teachings, and like a Catholic I was full of guilt. Nevertheless, I didn't care whom I stole from, what I did to family, or whom I hurt. Nothing at *all* pleased me more than a shot of dope. My first priority, my singleness of purpose, was to support my habit, by hook or crook.

Being an addict meant being ugly internally and externally and I didn't like that feeling, especially, when I'd the opportunity to look at myself, collect my thoughts, and reflect. I hope, by signing up for the prison's new therapeutic drug program, going through its screening, and accepted my life would change. Thus, I could once again be a whole person. I knew that as long as I was an addict, I'd never be whole. I'd always be the slave of the greatest con artist on earth, *heroin*.

The twenty-five of us accepted into the program, walked into an unstructured, undeveloped project, with four civilian counselors—outside staff. However, the four outside staff, left the entire structuring of the program in the hands of its twenty-five choice members.

On the first day, we met with the program staff, in the upper West Wing, of the new prison, and introduced ourselves. The staff gave us a quick bio of them and told us why they chose to be substance abuse counselors, especially, behind the walls. After a two-hours meeting, the staff left us at 11:00 a.m., on Friday morning with the assignment to building and structure a substance abuse program for heroin addicts.

By the time, Sunday night arrived and the last count of the day called out by blocks COs, "Count time, ten o'clock count time everybody in his room." The members from the group had already picked five group leaders, to lead them through the project. I was one of the five chosen for leadership, by the group, and the five of us chose "Project Overcome" as the project's name. Moreover, we decided that the project needed a project song, as well. Thus, we agreed that the group would open each morning meeting singing, "We Shall Overcome Someday."

Next thing we did were picked the five job status and mach each job status to a leader. I became the chief expediter while two other leaders became my assistant expediters. One of the other two picked became house manager and the other, program guru. My job and that of my two assistances were to make sure that members adhere to the rules and the order of the project.

Monday, the next morning, when the staff came in, they met first with the five leaders in the corridor's small library. There the program house manager, Jerry Funderburge, a best friend of mine, proudly opened a file folder sitting before him on the blond oak table, which we all sat around. He then removed copies of the project blueprint and passed each outside staff a copy.

After our staff meeting, we called a general meeting in one of the two game rooms and met with the rest of the project members to, further discuss the structuring and to tidy up loose ends. With that done, everyone stood up in a circle heal hands and sung, "We Shall Overcome Someday;" then, broke in to two-discussion group, and each group went into separate game room.

In the group while we arranged our chairs in a circle someone opened the windows, and the June air and fragrance of fresh mowed grass rushed into the room as if welcoming us on the first day of "dealing" with our drug problems. "Project Overcome" was all about us addicts "dealing" with our feelings, getting away from both our street names and our street images, working on our drug behavior, and sharing our experiences with one other. We brought up gut issues, and unhealed wounds that left us open and venerable to each other disdain.

Perhaps, because my being chief expeditor, I was called on first, by the group, to give an abbreviation of myself. I looked around somewhat shyly at the twelve members and three staff sitting in the circle. I opened by telling of my drinking wine at the age of thirteen; and how I went from drinking and smoking cigarettes to snorting nose inhalant, smoking pot, and drinking codeine-base cough syrup. Moreover, I told them by the end of my twenty-six birthday, I was a full-blown, heroin addict. I also conveyed to the group that eating sweets were my very first addiction, and that, that addiction begun in the toddler years of my life.

On December 12, 1971, after eighteen months, I graduated from the prison phase of Project Overcome, and paroled to the street's phase of the project, the "699 Halfway House," at 699 Massachusetts Avenue, one block from the Boston City Hospital, now called the Boston Medical Center. 699 Massachusetts Avenue was only one block away from the corner of North Hampton and Washington Street, now, the new drug scene and the place where my old buddies now hung out. The drug scene had begun changing location away from the *new* South End, to Lower Roxbury.

The "699" Halfway House was the final phase of the project and operated with outside staff, only. Each graduate released from Project Overcome Concord, stayed at 699 for three months, before their discharged into the community, while still on parole.

After two weeks of being stuck in the house on house-probation, Randy, one of the staff member, who was tiny and rather effeminate, with a kingside afro, large than that of Angel Davis, took a small group of us shopping. At Filenes' Basement department store I tried on a large black brimmed "super-fly" hat; and when I looked at myself in one of the walls' mirrors, I immediately lost all sight of the hard work I'd done on myself; because in that mirror, I perceived both my street and hustler's images looking back at me.

"Damn! Damn! I look good," I said to Mike Fitzgerald, one of the young members who stood next to me. Mike was a red head whose face forever looked as if it were sun burnt, winter or summer. He'd come from a nice home, manicure lawn, and two car garage. However, he'd got hold to some of that scag, or heroin, and got himself hooked. Mike went from using to selling heroin to support his habit; and like most of us, he was also servicing a five-year indefinite sentence.

"Elow," Mike said, "you're letting your old image seep back into your life. Don't let all those months you worked on your addiction get caught up, in that super-fly hat."

I respectfully thank him for his "pull-up"; yet continued admiring myself in the full-length mirror.

Pull-ups were something done by both outside staff and members of the project whenever they noticed another member or members reverting backward, to old junkie's ways. Pull-ups reminded members, in mischief, to think positive and stay inline with their growth and wellness. Moreover, the rule was that members wrote their pull-ups in the project logbook; then, Jerry, our house manager, read them to us at each morning meeting, where we discussed and judged each pull-up, according to its seriousness.

Just like that none of that mattered to me anymore, project rules or pull-ups, none of that; for as I admired myself in the mirror, with the black super-fly hat, cocked, on my head, I felt my yesterdays come rushing back at me in hot perused. Hence, from then on, I lost all sight of reality, reason, and most of all, the "dealing" I'd done on myself, overall. To quote Pushkin, "The old scenes carry on, at an accelerated pace."

In addition, yes, like a typical junky, I did leave 699 Massachusetts Avenue, allowing the beast of bad behavior to again, take control of my life. Thus, pulling me back into the abyss, where no common good existed. Living a life with heroin is repulsive and blinded to both modesty and decency. By leaving the house, not only was I a program failure, most like it I'd be a parole violated, too.

Ten days before Christmas, while most members were home on passes, I packed the few things I had into a brown shopping bag; and gently placed the super-fly upon my short, fresh haircut and gingerly circling the large rim of the hat, downward, with my right hand. Then, like a snail, I moved myself down four flights of dimly lighted stairs, passing the living room where a staff slept on the sofa. I continued down the stairs to the basement and out the cellar's back door into the chilly starlit December night.

The basement door let out into a parking lot where I felt the night chill mixed with freedom and empowerment sweep over me. Feeling like my own boss again, I stride down the long block up Massachusetts Avenue, to Washington Street hoping to run in to a dealer I knew who might give me a bag because he was glad to see me. Just one block away from 699 I fiend for the smell and the taste and the feel of heroin.

On the corner of Washington and Northampton Street, I entered Louis Lounge, one of Boston's favorite nightclubs where the best people hung out.

Nevertheless, once and a while, after 1:00 a.m., when the corners had quieted down, you might find a dealer lurking in the dim lighted lounge. However, there were only a hand full of people sitting at the bar watching television.

As I turned to leave, I waved at one of the guys I barely knew and stepped out the door. I then crossed Washington Street and entered Big Jim Shanty Lounge. There I found it empty except for the bar tender and the lounge's boss—Big Jim Shanty—who sat at the bar drunk, drooling on his clothes and looking like a fat Humpty Dumpty with money stuffed into each pocket. Big Jim was a mob and no one, not even a sick junky would pick his pockets. Moreover, he was quite a decent man to the Black folks, in and around the neighborhoods.

Outside I took a left turn on Northampton Street and promenaded down to Tremont Street where I'd flag a cab. However, in the middle of the block a police cruiser slowly pull up along side of me and stopped.

"What you got in the bag?" the cop in the passenger seat interrogated, as he rolled down his window, reveling his round white face, paled from the lack of summer sunlight.

"My clothes," I dryly answered.

"Look to me like you broke in somebody house or car?" cracked the driver, bending toward the passenger's window to get a better look at me.

"They're mines," I replied giggling inside of me because I'd done nothing wrong and there was nothing they could do to me even if they knew I'd left the program. There was no crime committed in leaving the program. Moreover, it was up to my parole officer to violate my parole or not. So tonight the cops could do all the questioning they wanted to; for I was clean, thus far.

"Where you gone?" exclaimed pale face.

"Home."

"Where's home?"

"JP."

"Okay, go on."

"Hay, would you guys give me a ride," I asked, knowing they'd say no and think me audacious for asking, which I was.

"Give you a ride! A ride where?" the driver uttered, while his white face looked at me, dumbfounded, which look as if it were the frowning theatre mask.

"What the hell you think we are? We're not the"T," asshole!" cracked pale face.

"You gots lots of balls, I give you that much—"

"You want to go to jail?" the driver snapped. "That's the only ride you get from us."

With that, I backed away from the cruiser, snickered to myself and preceded toward Tremont Street, as the cop's car rolled slowly past me.

It was 2:00 a.m., an hour and a half after leaving 699, when I stuck my keys into the locks, and open the door to our apartment, and Marcia being a mother and light sleeper heard me come in.

"Who is that!" she bellowed from her bedroom hoping it's not an intruder.

"It's just me, honey," I whispered, making my way through the small corridor, to our bedroom, hoping the kids slept through Marcia's shout.

Like always, the house was cleaned and orderly; and the houseplants that hung in the living room windows green and vibrant, while the carpet on the floor gave off a lilac fragrant, as if just washed.

In one voice Marcia retorted, "Elow! you walking on my washed carpet and I just know you still in the program and not on the run; don't tell me you already left the program!" she exclaimed.

" Sheee, you'll wake the kids—"

"Don't tell me nothing about the kids, because if you cared for them you'd have a job and be at home with us, instead of in-and-out of prison all the time!"

We could now hear the kids getting up and going to the bathroom, as if they needed to go. Pam was the first one to past our room on her way to the bathroom. I gave her a wave and closed our bedroom door; then, went and sat on the edge of the bed while Marcia remained standing.

"Elow, tell me you still in the program where you were doing so well. The kids and me were happy and I just kept telling them you'd be home for good soon. Like always, you let us down again, because I know you left—I can feel it. I can tell by that damn hat you got on your head. "Why you leave, Elow?" When, you were doing so well."

"The staff," I said, hurrying my words, "at 699 had put me in the 'dog house' for argument with one of the staffs there because he didn't appreciate the way I'd cleaned the bathrooms and told me to do them over. I told him that if he didn't like my work, do it himself. For that, the house staff met and decided to stick me into the, dog house for ten days, and stripped of my Christmas pass. That meant I wouldn't be home with you and the kids for Christmas, so I left."

"How do they think you going to change," Marcia uttered, as she came and sat on the bed near me, "by keeping you away from your family, especially on the holidays. What's wrong with them?"

My junky lies had softened Marcia a bit. However, I don't think she bought it, but like always, she let it pass with the dream that this time I'd get a job and we'd have a happy life.

Marcia wore a leopard-patterned nightgown that draped over her lovely shoulders showing a modest amount of cleavage. I gently pulled her up from the bed as I stood, and drew her body to mines she held back and lifted the gown over her head removing it; then, undressed me.

The next morning I awoke early and called Reverent Michael Haynes, a sitting member of the Massachusetts State Parole Board, and pastor of the Twelve Baptist Church in Roxbury. The pastor picked up the phone on its first ring. "Hello," a calmly voice answered.

With my heart feeling as though it were beating in my throat, I managed to say trying to sound innocent, "Reverent Haynes, my name is Oren Elow, and recently you and the parole board members paroled me from Project Overcome at Concord, to 699 Massachusetts Avenue.

"Yes, yes, I remembered you. A name like Oren Elow isn't easy to forget. "What can I do for you Mr. Elow?" Reverent Haynes asked.

I gave the pastor the same excuse for leaving the program I'd given Marcia; and like her, I knew that he didn't totally believe me. For in his line of work, he's heard all kinds of stories coming from the mouths of both prisoners and parishioners. Nevertheless, he patiently listened to me; then, told me to call the Project Overcome parole board officer and explain to him what happened. Reverent Haynes, a short, small, and black-skinned man remained as calm as a guru and promised me he'd call him as well. Moreover, he also promised that if I got into any trouble at all, he'd make sure himself, that I went back to prison on parole violation. The complete time my being on the phone, Marcia stood near and now felt better, that the pastor had promise to speak to my parole officer in my behalf.

I never did keep the appointment I'd made with the Project Overcome parole officer, who I promised to see right after Christmas. For right after Christmas, I went, right back to using heroin and pulling B&Es—breaking into people homes. Common sense would have made a New Year, 1972, resolution to change my lifestyle. However, addicts don't do things out of common sense, they do things out of fear; and that fear comes from within. Moreover, addicts aren't strong people. They cannot cope with the slightest anxieties, the slightest fears; or the slightest rejections from others; and so their neurotic, addicted behavior causes them to uses dope to candy-coat those fears. Every addict has his own set of fears and anxiety, which can be many and diverse.

Getting high on heroin is a get-well, feel good, quick fit; it was my contentment, my psychiatric medication. It was comfortable and its loftiness placed me in total bliss. Nothing seems to disturb me when I was in a heroin frame of mind. For my fears and anxieties were temporarily place in check.

Most addicts are good and gracious people and come from all races and classes. Heroin cares nothing about the lives of the addicts' class, or race, or their statuses or where they live, or come from. Heroin just wants to have a good time and want the addicts to come out and play no matter the mood of weather, and while promising addicts joy and peace, heroin suffocates them between life and death.

Being addicted to heroin like being in love with a foxy woman, whom you know in your guts it isn't good for you, yet you continue to hold on to her because her sex is explosive. She throws her lusty body at the junky and says, "That's right honey do it and tell mama you love it. The junky nods deep rubs his face with the palm of his right hand and said, "I love it baby." When I was high, neither my anxieties nor my compulsive behaviors fazed me, I felt empowered, in control, hmph. It gave me a bold certainly and a dare devil attitude. I'd often pondered the thoughts of how a drug like heroin could so gracefully relieve both the addicts' anxieties and life's pains, leaving them elated. Yet, it was scandalous and deadly.

I knew, not long after my addiction that heroin was a pain in the butt, because the elated feeling it gave me came with an agonizing price. In order to support my habit, I had to lower my head to the ground like a sniffing dog. I lied, cheated, and stole; yes, even from my family and love ones. I once broke into the home of one of the state parole board members and uncountable other notable peoples. If I was dope sick, I either got money for my fix, or ended up busted trying to pull, a B&E to get it. All my body knew, when dope sick, was that it needed a fill-up to buildup. It needed to get off "E," emptiness. No way was I going home sick. I'd get the money somewhere, or go to prison, or to my death trying.

In January '73, the system discharged me from Concord after serving nine-months for parole violation and program failure. Again, the same day of my release, I began using heroin; however, this time I got on the Boston City Hospital methadone program. By being on the methadone program, I didn't have to worry about being dope sick. However, a large amount of junkies on the methadone program still used heroin and other illicit drugs, too. Lots of illicit pills taking and alcohol drinking went hand-in-hand with the junky's methadone program. A Junky is a junky is a junky.

Because of my being on the methadone program Marcia, the children, and I began doing a lot more thing together as a family. We took long drives and engaged in picnics on summer holidays. Sometimes we didn't even know where we would picnic. We'd just got into the car, and perhaps, the car would turn west and we'd found ourselves on the Mohawk Trail as far as Orange, Massachusetts looking for an ideal green space to picnic, where the flow of water from a small brook rushes downward, beneath the trees and bushes toward its purpose.

Other times we found ourselves picnicking on the edge of the Cape Cod Canal near the Sagamore Bridge, hoping to see a whale, in the water, for once and a while, one might mosey into the canal. There were times when we didn't leave the city at all, we simply drove a few blocks to the *emerald necklace*, at Franklin Park, laid out the blanket and unloaded the Bar B. Q. pit, the children's games, and our foodstuff. There the kids had vast amount of greenery to hit golf balls and play their other childless games.

They were happy and showed it in their chatting, laughter and fooling around; and all I could do was wish that I could be a wonderful father and a decent husband. However, it forever stayed a wish, for heroin whispered in my ear—don't even think of it. The kids also love the beachside amusement parks, thus most Sundays the family drove to one of the amusements park-beaches.

Since Theresa and Darryl were the oldest, they just wanted to do their own thing. Therefore, when we arrived at a beachside amusement park, they would disappear into the crowd, and checking back with us as the day flowed on, or when they ran out of money. None of the children cared for the ocean, then, so swimming was out of the games.

Nevertheless, they had no problem spending up money on fun and game. Even as a fulltime junky, I never hesitated giving my children what they needed materially when I was around. However, it was love they wanted. I stole enough money to support my habit and family, and drive a BMW. Nevertheless, there were times when I had not a penny.

"Mama, Daddy!" Pam teased, "Come ride the roller coaster with Gwenette and me."

"No thanks," Marcia and I'd answered together. The kids knew that we were both terrified of the roller coaster. Our thing, were playing the selections of games—on the ground.

We were happy, and I was having a grand time and staying out of prison, for in 1970s, money filled from the sky for me. I was making my living selling diamonds, gold, silver, and valuable coins, which came from B&Es; this not counting the mounds of cash.

However, little by little I begun cheeping away at heroin, like once or twice a week and before I realized it, like a panther in a tree heroin sprung upon me with the quickness and I developed both a methadone and heroin habit. The family good times went out the window and I was back again yelling and screaming, and shooting dope like a mad man. I felt like a scum, weak and not welling to face up to manhood, my responsibility to wife and children. I had a good wife and health loving children; however, heroin was my master and I did as ordered.

EIGHT

MADNESS at WALPOLE STATE PRISON

On one of those days when the sky was clearly blue, sunny, and April, 1977, I plea bargained, to a B&E, before Judge James Donahue, in Suffolk Superior Court, who then sentenced me to serve six to ten years at Walpole State Prison, now called "Cedar Junction." I'd finally made it to the "big house," the "hill," the "white house." as the convicts called Walpole. However, I had already heard a great deal about the violence and murderous reputation that Walpole hosted; I had no fear, for many of my boys whom I knew from the street were there. Moreover, it wasn't my first time among convicts.

There were three of us sentenced to Walpole, that day, by the same Suffolk Superior Court judge Donahue that clear sunny, April morning. Both prisoners—Kaahna Ahadia and John Terrance were also friends of mine.

Kaahna, also called Weasel because of his slender supple body and weasel ways. Weasel was quite a character. He was smooth and precise in his coolness. He walked as if walking on glass barefooted, slow and gingerly; and had a chronic habit of wiggling the fingers of both hands, which he kept at his side, as he amble along. He did everything with trend. Yeah, Kaahna was the essence of hipness and practiced both Yoga and Transcendental Meditation. In a plea-bargaining, for armed robbery, he was sentence to serve twelve to fifteen years.

John Terrance, who we called Motor Car because of his reputation for stealing cars, was only seventeen years old and the youngest among the three of us. He'd pleaded out to something like Seventeen years, for a sequence of store robberies while armed. The three of us were also heroin addicts, and we all lived and hung out in Jamaica plain Housing Project.

At Walpole, the booking "screw"—or guard—placed the three of us in one of the intake-holding cells to await booking and medical examination. We laughed and joke and had flashbacks about our yesterdays; and no one seemed to care that we'd ended up in a bloodletting zoo. One-by-one the booking guard called us into the booking room and once called, we didn't return to the intake cell. They saved me for last.

After my booking that consisted of fingerprinting, photos, answering bio questions, given a con-number W36070, and seeing the prison doctor. A serious faced young screw, neatly dressed in his khaki uniform and wearing a fresh blond crew-cut haircut, escorted me from the hospital, into a lengthy, empty corridor with a high polished tile floor. The corridor was well lighted and slightly intimidating.

After passing the gym, school, chapel, auditorium, and mess hall, we moved passed "inner control," where three guards worked controls that controlled the interior of the prison; from behind, a bubble made of bulletproof glass.

"Damn! This is a sure enough prison," I said mouthing off, as we continue up the corridor and into the maximum-security section of the prison.

"Where did you think you were going, to a youth detention?" The young guard retorted, as he approached three tough looking screws, dressed in black fatigue and wearing combat both, sitting at a desk placed in the center of the maximum-security corridor.

"Why he's gone to block-2," said one the screws, "when he's a new man?"

"He supposes to go in the probation unit," a miniature built screw with a light, blond afro responded.

"I was told by booking that he got into a fist fight at the jail holding him for his transfer here," the young guard said. "Guess they want to watch him for a few days."

"Will, block-2 sure hold him," said one of the screws, polishing his black combat booths.

"You can't judge a book by its color," answered another. "He don't even look like he belong here."

Color, I thought.

There were nine blocks in the max end; moreover, cellblock "nine" once used for Death Row, before the state of Massachusetts abolished its death penalty. Therefore, all prisoners on the row, wound up with a life sentence without parole. Though Death Row was now empty of prisoners, it still hosted the electric chair.

My escort and I stopped in front of cellblock 2—know as "max two." He called out to the block guard; and we heard the guard drag his chair backwards on the concrete floor and grunted as he lift himself. The fat belly cellblock screw dragged him self to the door yarning and said, "Red! I see you got another max inmate for me, huh?"

"Yeah, there's always another one, or two, or five. They just keep popping in and out," Red said.

"They keep me in a job," the block screw said, as he unlocked the herculean navy gray painted, steel barred door, with a large flat key, from a ring of other large flat keys, that he kept hooked to his belt.

The block screw was an old timer, in his mid sixties and ready for retirement. However, at that age in order to work the max-end, he had to have had convict trust and respect, or else the cons would have ran his ass out the block, as they'd done so many others screws.

I stood at the desk as the two screws exchanged papers, and couldn't believe what I was seeing. The once gray painted walls in the cellblock, was cake with human feces, rotten food, or any other foul and filth that might stick to the walls. The cons in conflict with the administration about one rule or another, had literally taken there own waste and had then thrown it out of their cell door on to the walls and flat. In front me, the flat littered with rotten food, Styrofoam plates and cups; white plastic spoon, burnt pillows, blankets, sheets, and yes human feces.

Instantly I felt entombed, and it seemed as though my *Kundalini*K had rushed up my spinner cord and flooded my head with, head aching anxieties. My entire body felt weighty and I could have sworn that I'd lost my hearing for a few second or more. Then, in a flash, I for the first time noticed just how noises the maximum-security section was. In the cellblock, prisoners yelled from cell to cell, radios and televisions blearing, and the smell of rotten food, human feces, and marijuana filled the air in cell block-2.

No prisoners would sweep or clean the blocks in the maximum-security section of the prison where Walpole housed its hardened convicts; and those convicts mission were to do as much damage to the prison cellblocks as possible. The convicts' prison theme was "make them pay." In other words, the more damage done to the prison by the cons the more money the system, shelled out for cost and label.

The convicts figured if they done enough damage to Walpole, the system would run out of money; then, forced to close it down. They were trying to shut the 'big house" down, however, they never prevail. Nevertheless, the cons did get the system to change its name from Walpole, to "Cedar Junction." The reason for the name change happened because Walpole prisoners, at that time, murdered each other on regular bases.

Thus, the citizens in the town of Walpole became nauseated with the high prison murder rate, happening in their town district, and wanted no relationship with prisoners or prison. Hence, the town forced the governor of the Commonwealth of Massachusetts to change the prison's name to "Cedar Junction." Nonetheless, today people still call it—Walpole.

Most prisoners confined to the max blocks, were there for anything from possessing drugs, caught with a shank—makeshift prison made knife, fighting, and other violence against either inmate or screw. Some of the prisoners were psychotics and out of control, while others behaved as if they walked on all four. Moreover, the theme, "make them pay" included anything that could damage or demoralize the prison, including murder. Most of the stabbings and murders stemmed from a drug deals gone bad, beefs over money owed, sport gaming, and stitching.

As I waited for the two screws to end their chat, I heard Red tell the block officer that he was going into the Massachusetts state police in a few months, and that he couldn't wait to put on their uniform. Just then, I felt eyes staring at me. Cons on the flat had stuck their mirrors out of their cell door sizing me up and curious to see, who the new man.

When Red left the block, the block officer finally gave me my gears, which set on the desk all the time they talked: One heavy green army blanket, two sets of sheet, two sets of pillowcases, two bath towels, and my cell number. As I made my way up the steel stairs, color "grey" and narrow tier, color "grey" to my cell on the third and top tier color "grey," the earsplitting noise coming from convicts radios and televisions; and the yelling back and forth from cell-to-cell vibrated the tier beneath my feet. I thought that if I suffered death in the "pole," noise would be the criminal.

My cell number, forty-five was the last cell on the tier and that meant I had to past forty-four others, each occupied by a prisoner. As I made my journey to the other end of the tier, I passed cells where some cons took naps, others cooked food in their tiny hot pots, and as they stirred their cooking, they yelled from cell-to-cell, clowning around and talking about some chick they once knew in the street, or something like that. Some did push-ups, and some stood at their door and greeted me with, "what's happening?" Other laid on there bunk, watching their blaring black and white, thirteen inch, TV while they also listened to their screaming radio.

However, in the cell before mines, in number 44, stood a short, stocky, shinny-face, purple-black skinned con about five, five with a Goliath built. Moreover, the con talked to him self and had a small magazine cutout picture, of Muhammad ALI, pasted to his forehead.

"Hay brother where you from? I know you!"

"Jamaica Plain, JP," I said as I glanced at his bear chest built thick and hard from years of lifting weight. With my cell still locked, I had to wait until the screw in the "trap" open it electronically.

"I know lots of people in J. P.," he excitingly said. "Hay, 'ah 'ah, brother you like Muhammad Ali?"

"He's the man—"

"Yea, yea, brother you know what I mean," he said slapping his forehead so hard that it sounded like a loud handclapped. "That's why he come out my head to let them tuff guys know not to f… with, Tom Brown!"

"No brother, not you," he said, passing me his rock-hard hand to shake; "I wouldn't do nothin' to you; but some of them black spades and white honkies and screws need to get f… up, too. That's why Tom Brown in max end, for bustin' up one of them young punk screw. Those young punks think they can disrespect Tom Brown. They know they got to respect Tom Brown, or get f… up."

I didn't let on, however, I knew of Tom from when we were in Concord together a few years ago. By the time, the screw opened my cell door and locked me in number forty-five it was a little after 11:00 p. m., and we didn't get out of our cell until after lunch the following afternoon. We ate both breakfast and lunch in them. In addition, with our two boiled eggs, two slices of toast, a pint of milk, a teaspoon of butter, and a cup of coffee for breakfast, I also got a ton of earsplitting noise as well. With rotten food and excrement, covering the flat, most cons, at recreation, hung out on the two tiers, or in the cell of their Pals. A group, with their back against the tier's railing, smoked some pot while others gathered up in cells shooting up.

However, the prisoners who remained in their cell to nap slept on their mattress placed on the floor, for they used their bunk to barricading themselves inside their cell. The sleepers placed their heavy iron bunk upright against their open cell doors; then, placed both metal desk and chair against the bunk to prevent anyone from entering while they slept. The bunk was so heavy that if someone tried entering a napping prisoner's cell, he would first have to move the heavy bunk out of the way; causing the heavy metals to drag across the concrete floor, which would hopefully alert the sleeper, that's if he wasn't drugged up.

Nevertheless, really, if another prisoner wanted to get at a sleeper, all he needed to do was take a Molotov cocktail, made of lighter fluid sold in the canteen or gasoline swiped from mechanic school, and throw the makeshift bomb into the cell. Lighter fluid and gasoline were as lethal as a prison made shank. Nevertheless, the shank was the weapon of practice and widely used at Walpole.

Beside the porcelain sink that was broken, at its top between the two faucets, yet still in working condition, my cell was tidy and the porcelain toilet usable. However though, what intrigued me was the large mural painted on the wall over my cell's door. A prisoner, I suppose, who was perhaps serving life or a drag out long sentence, in hope of getting out, had painting the scene of a bunk, covered with a green military blanket and made militarily tight. The bunk sat in a gruesome looking tunnel where the walls on either side casted a darkish grey clouded hue. The tunnel, gradually became brighter and brighter as it made its expedition towards the far exit, where a burst of yellow sunshine, awaited. My objective was for me to do my time as tightly made as the bunk in the mural and pass through the burst of yellow sunshine, into freedom. Moreover, like good art, the mural had also found its way into the coffer of my mind.

I remained at maximum-security Walpole for about six months; housing in both maximum and minimum end, while working in the "plate shop," making license plates for the state of Massachusetts, before my transfer to Norfolk.

Once inside the population at Norfolk, a minimum-security, and a sight away from Walpole, I hooked up with, Stanley Jones, a close friend of mines, and Joe Sales, a friend of Stanley. Stanley was a stick-up artist and robbed mostly drug stores to feed his heroin addiction, and now serving a lengthily stretch for a drug store stick-up. Joe Sales was a dope supplier from Harlem and doing time for trafficking in heroin. Now the two of them were running a federal funded drug prevention program—"Yesterday Today and Tomorrow," within the prison's wall.

Then, Joe Sales was its director of program, Stanley its director of treatment; and two weeks after my arrival at Norfolk, I was hired as YTT "drug educational" counselor—for I had the knowledge. When at Concord, had I not helped with developing Project Overcome, from blueprint, with its own halfway house in Boston? I'd also gathered an education in drug prevention and psychotherapy while there as one of Project Overcome's staffs and clients.

My job was to hold four nightly classes in the prison school building, teaching YTT inmate clients the danger of licit and illicit drugs and their effects. Teaching these classes educated the clients about how different drugs had different influences on the body and mind, and what could happen if abused. We studied the danger of the drugs most practiced by addicts and drug users at that time, in the 1970s: Opiate and its derivates like heroin; alcohol, LSD, cocaine, peyote, mushrooms, and pills from stimulants to barbiturates.

At the end of the three months course, the class graduated with certificates in drug education; and there after a new class commenced. The uniqueness of YTT was that "all" its counselors were Norfolk inmates, and each paid a hundred dollars a month. At any given time, YTT had thirty-five to forty clients in its program, with an inmate staff of eight, who counselor their clients, using the therapeutic group-sessions concept.

I'd been at Norfolk for some six months when the prisoners in my housing unit, 2-2, asked me to run for unit representative. Norfolk had an "inmate council," which consisted of an executive board, two inmate chairpersons, one Black the other White, a secretary and a representative at large. The body of council consisted of eighteen unit representatives, and eighteen unit alternate representatives. Thus, each of the eighteen housing unit, at Norfolk, was represented with both a representative and an alternate.

The inmate council owned the inmate populace canteen, two inmate laundries, and the business of recycling both soda cans and bottles. The revenue from council businesses went into the administration inmate fund. Moreover, the money bought law books and copying machines for the law library. As well, the money bought microwave ovens, electric frying pans, and cooking utilities for each unit. It also paid for the inmate music and recreational equipments—and some Christmases each prisoner received a five-dollar canteen voucher from the council. Nevertheless, the warden had the final say on how much money the council draw from its inmate's fund. However, he usually Okayed our requests.

NINE

THE NORFOLK TWENTY-SEVEN

The year 1978, and I'd been at Norfolk about a year. When on a scorching mid August afternoon the Inmate council called a special meeting to discuss what should be done about the way in which prisoners' visits were continually harassed and striped-search by screws claiming to be looking for contraband. The screws often and randomly took inmates' visitors into a small room and stripped them of their clothing. It mattered not who or what age the visitors were, ninety-nine years old or a toddle.

The guards didn't care, hell, they'd make a poor old, gray-skinned shrunken Nana strip, and would strip the cute tubby little toddle, too. However, the inmates' patients to stop their dear ones from the harassments and the shame of a skin-shake, stripped down buck-naked, were at a boiling point. They were angry and ready for mutiny.

The council on few occasions had spoken to the warden on the matter. In fact, a group of twelve prisoners including Stanley Jones, now YTT director, and me had some months earlier taken over the prison's library; and had refused returning to our units until the warden took the inmates request seriously about stopping the stripping of visitors.

After spending the night in the library, the next morning the warden met with us to discuss our sit-in and contentions. During the two hours of converse we explained to the warden that he must look at the facts that our visitors weren't the ones' doing time and shouldn't be going through the stress of being striped like convicts. The inmates felt it was pure harassment by the institution, and it had to stop. We suggested, instead of visitors randomly stripped, rather strip every prisoner leaving the visiting room. We were saying strip each prisoner upon leaving the visiting room and not just a few; and if there's any contraband found on the prisoner, then bust the inmate and his visit. *What so hard about that,* I thought.

The warden, Michael Fare, promised to straighten out the problem, and agreed not to take any displinarary action, against the twelve of us if we promised to return to our units. We knew when we took over the library that there was a great possibility that we might in up back in Walpole. It really was the roll of the dices.

The warden didn't at all hold up to his promise, because visitors were still being stripped; and that in fact caused the prisoners to flam-up with disdain. So, at the special meeting the Norfolk Inmate Council unanimously voted to call a work stoppage, a strike, a take over; however, in a peaceful way. All work done by prisoners inside and outside the wall of Norfolk would be discontinued which meant the prison's industry that grossed millions of dollars a year would have to shut its doors.

The industry that made furniture, which you can still find, today, underneath the golden dorm, at the State House, courthouses, and all over Massachusetts legal system, would have to shut its doors. Moreover, the industry made manhole covers, trash containers for both state and city use. In addition, it made prisoners' garb, mattresses, and printed all the stationary the administration needed for the running of the institution. The inmates would no longer keep the upkeep of the administration building, hospital, and kitchen.

All the work that the prisoners once did would come to an absolute stop. Moreover, the entire Norfolk administration staff would now have to do the work the inmates once did, which would put a herculean strain on the entire Massachusetts Department of Correction; for they certainly would have to bring in other staffs from other institutions to lend a hand. Hell, someone had to cook the food and feed the prisoners … and be ready for what ever jumped off. Before this issue was over with, we were going to see more uniformed security personal inside the wall than you'd see at a police academe.

Before the strike, the council had to get both the black and white population to put aside their pettiness, black versa white and vice versa, attitude and come together on the visiting grievances since the stripping of visitors affected everyone's visit. Both race embraced each other, and the beat went on.

Every inmate who got visits could relate to the embarrassment and dehumanizing their love ones went through when told to strip, ghastly! Therefore, it wasn't too difficult for the units representatives to get the entire Norfolk prison population to come together and support a peaceful work stoppage.

"Okay! Open your mouth!" a screw would bark at visitors when strip searching them. "Now take off your dress." The mouth is checked and the dress is search for drug and other contraband; then, tossed on top a small wood table that shines from wear down, and years of screws tossing stripped clothing upon it. "Now remove your bra and panties; those are so also casted onto the table when searched. Now lift your breast, turn around, bend forward and spread your butt … with your hands," the screw bends and investigates the woman cavities and that of the male visits. The poor baby is totally undressed and dipper removed …

The next morning when the work-whistle blow at, 9:00 a.m., sounding like a steamboat blowing off steam. Prisoners akin to ants exited their housing unite not for work, but to begin marching around the green manicured quad where ten redbrick buildings surrounding it was designed similar to the "Harvard Yard." When the guards noticed the mass movement of prisoners quietly marching around the quad, they knew it was the beginning of some kind of protest.

Not one screw came out any of the buildings they were minding to shout their regular: "What's going on? Move on move on, you heard the work-whistle!" In fact, they now said nothing to prisoners. Even the Institutional Police Service, the IPS, the tough screws, the special police force, who not only policed the prisoners, but the correctional officers as well, said nothing.

Ever morning when the work-whistled blew the prisoners could rely on seeing the IPS roaming the quad and randomly patting down prisoners looking for contraband. However, on the morning of the strike, as soon as they themselves notice that no one were going to work they forthwith discontinue their harassment of prisoners and moved quickly off the quad into their station, which occupied a tiny section of school building's first floor.

While prisoners marched, the inmate council met in the council's room and office at the inmate social building, to execute its plan. The council had its own telephone system, the old switchboard style, with a direct line to the outside world. All we needed to do was dial the switchboard from the council's room and one of the two inmates working the board, in the administration building, would connect use to our calls. We took turns, working the phone: notifying families and friends, prison activist groups, and members of the state legislatures ... Our objective was to reach out to as many people in the street as possible, before the administration thought of shutting down both the council and the inmate's phone system.

We were lucky, for either, the administration didn't take the strike seriously at first, or they'd forgotten to shut down the phones system. Nevertheless, whatever their plans were we had three-days of open phones communications before the warden order them cut off.

The administration now understood that the prisoners weren't going back to work until they received from the warden, a legal written document promising that their visitors would no longer be harassed, disrespected, or searched when visiting.

In addition, by late afternoon, on the third day of the strike, some of our families and friends, along with the media and community activist groups, were already outside the prison wall: In the prison's parking lot, honk, honking their horns and howling, so that all prisoners behind the wall heard them. The support, outside the high voltage thirty-foot wall gave prisoners a gust of wind, which pushed their faith persistently toward their contentions.

Lawmakers from the State House, whom we'd gotten in touch with, were calling the administration, wanting to know what the 'hell' was going on at Norfolk. In addition, the news media had begun broadcasting our strike on both TV and radio; and the prison population and inmate council were enchanting on how well thing had gone in such a short time. So far, our plans were working well. However, on the forth morning of the protest, I was awakening by a knock on my door, then, Peanut stuck his tiny head inside.

"Man," I growled. "What you want?"

"Elow," Peanut softly said, as if not wanting to awake anyone. "They out there, Elow, the state troopers, man; they're out there. They got the whole place surrounded. The quad full of them!"

"Man gets your ass out of my room with that stuff!" Through half opened eye, I peeked at my Seiko watch, which I never remove from my wrist, the whole time I spent in prison. "Come on Pea, man; it's not even six o'clock in the morning yet—"

"No joke, Elow, they out there, and they're everywhere around the quad. Just get up and look."

Peanut, no taller than five-foot four and looked like a PeeWee Harman, lived across the hall from me, with his room facing the quad. Norfolk didn't have cells, the had small rooms with unlocked doors, which we came out at well.

"Let see," I said, as I got out of bed and slipped into my slippers, not bothering to remove the marijuana that was hidden in the sole of the left slipper, and crossed over to Peanut's room. Inside the tiny room, I had to turn sideways to avoid brushing against the foliage of Peanut's avocado plant, I should say small tree that he had grown from its seed. In the window hung a huge vivacious spider plant, with innumerable baby plants hanging from its many steams, resembling umbilical cords. I gently moved the steams aside and peeped out onto the quad from the second floor.

"Damn man! you're right, they're out there!" I exclaimed, as I spun to leave, my lungs battling in my chest as if looking for a way out so that it might suck in air. There were about twenty state troopers, with hats lowered just above their brow and uniform so orderly they seemed as though they had been, tailored to their bodies. The troopers stood spread eagle stiff, surrounding the quad and each holding a riot shut gun across his chest.

I hurried back to my room nearly knocking over the avocado plant. In my room, I began feeling good about what we were doing. For the strikers contention against the prison system was working; and I was part of making it work. I felt quite keyed up to see just how well the theatrical would play out.

One thing for sure, conflict was involved. As I sat to use the toilet, with the window opened, something I did each morning like clockwork, I pull out one of the four joints hidden in my slipper. Lit it, took a long drag and choked into a coughing fit. I took a shorter drag, swallowed the smoke, sniffed some air into my lungs, and the pot high was on. I sat there some minutes, thinking about what state troopers did to prisoners when they entered an unrest prison. Convicts said that they came in like mad men, cracking skulls, tear gassing, and destroying inmates' property.

The troopers never did gas or rough up anyone. In fact, they never enter a single unit. They stood tall and intimidating on the quad and two prison years. While correctional officers from Massachusetts four other state prisons, Walpole, Norfolk, Concord, and Bridgewater state prisons did the lugging, the work of retrieving the prison. In addition, the prison managerial staffs, the prison civilian workers, and the screws would now do the dirty work around the prison the inmates were doing a few days ago.

There were five separate groups of screws, or goons, about twelve to a group dressed in swap green fatigues. They had no guns only belly clubs and handcuffs; and from our windows, we could see goon squads marching in military formation, along the quad, clobbering their belly clubs against their gloved hands, in a sign of intimidation. Whack, whack, whack; one, two, three, four, they marched entering units and exiting with prisoner or prisoners they went in to get; then, haul them down the quad towards the administration building. Some of the prisoners lugged from their units wore only underwear and maybe shoes, while others were fully dressed or partly dressed.

When we saw the men in green near our unit, 2-2, we all fled to our rooms like mice and became quitter than silent. When they finally entered, we heard their heavy combat-booths striking on the tile floor as they marched toward the housemen section of the unit, which was on the first floor, near the kitchen.

"Get up!" We heard a goon demanding from downstairs.

If any prisoner was still asleep, he was certainly playing possum. For a few minutes or so, we heard nothing. It seemed a though every prisoner in 2-2, was holding his breath. It seemed as if all had come to a stand still. However, again, we heard movement. The goons were now proceeding up the stairs to the second floor, where I populated, whacking their club against the steel, hand railing, while trudging up the stairs with their high polished booths.

The goon squad marched right up to my door and stopped. The door then flow opened, and when two goons stepped into the room, I felt as if my heart had paused, the first goon held a body length Plexiglas shield in front of him, while the other goons waited in the doorway, combat ready, just in case I acted up. I who was now sitting on the edge of my made bed watching Good Morning America and wearing only my watch and boxers and trying to look as innocent as possible. Like a third grader facing his father for bad grades.

"Get off the bed and strip!" uttered one of the goons who stood behind the shield carrier. I took off my underwear and slowly passed it to the screw standing near the screw with the shield, trying not to do anything that might cause the goons to used force. I certainly didn't want to end up a Bloody Mary. "Stoop and spread your butt checks, you know the drill; take off your watch and put it on the table, now your slipper."

At that point, I passed him the slippers and held my breath. I knew that I had to remain cool and thank goodness, the goon really just looked at the two slippers, and dropped them onto the floor. The slipper with the pot felled face down, and I thought sure that the three joints in them had slipped out, however, they stayed put. After skinned searched me, I was told to put on my drawers.

"May I put on my shoes instead?" I politely inquired. Hell, I didn't want the slippers because the next prison I was lug to might surely find the marijuana.

"Put on what I tell you put on!" the screw doing the searching grumbled.

Yes sir boss, I said to myself. I was then shackled wrists and ankles by two other goons who had been standing in the corridor and removed from my room.

"Okay, let's go!" barked the two goons simultaneously, as they grabbed me by both my arms—one on either side of me.

Outside I could see other prisoners, across the quad, shackled and lugged towards the administration building. However, the August heat and humidity didn't seem to bother the state troopers who stood tall and in readiness. There were also a couple goons following us with cameras as they hurried me down the quad. I disregarded the order the goons gave me not to talk, and asked politely, "Where did you say I'm going?"

"We don't know," whispered one of the goons holding on to my right arm. "Now shut up."

With the cameras still rolling the goons, marched me down the dim lighted corridors, in the administration building, with their high polished floors, however, they were now scuffed from the morning foot traffic and not maintained since the strike began. We passed through the trapdoors, which lead us to "out of control" where screws working behind a bulletproof glass panels looked at me with broad smiles on their faces, as if to say, man, you're in trouble now.

Outside, the wall, in the parking lot, before our eyes were parked a caravan of blue prisons' transportation buses and vans. Once outside the goons transferred me to a group of screws who scuttled me off to one of the vans waiting in line. Already sitting in the hot, stuffy van was Tally Davis, a drug addict and heroin supplier from Harlem, serving five-years and a day for possession and distribution of heroin. On the bench across from Tally was Charles 2X McDonald also from Harlem; serving natural life without parole for killing a pimp in Boston's Combat Zone.

2X had already been in prison some seven years now, and was in tip-top-shape from jogging, boxing lifting iron, and his dark skinned face glowed with health. No matter his mood, he always depicted good humor. In fact, he started laughing as soon as he saw the screws help lift me into the van because I seemed to have a problem climbing the one-step with the ankle- chine.

I'd met 2X in Walpole, before I was sent to Norfolk, and we became instant friends. I know, that we both knew, that it was no better time to be in each other company then now. The other prisoner setting juxtaposed to Tally was Paul Little from Boston Combat Zone, also serving a life sentence, with out parole, for murder. Paul reminded me of a Paul Bunyan of a fellow, big with blond hair and profound blue eyes.

When in the street Paul hung out in the Combat Zone, Boston "red light district" playing gangster, hustler, and ladies' man. It was his gangster attitude that got him a natural life sentence. By the time our van pulled out of Norfolk's parking lot, there were six of us in it—stuffy and hot, from sitting in the hot August sun.

"Hay officer!" Tally uttered, talking through the small grated window that separated the prisoners from the two screws in the van's cab. "Where we gone?"

"Now Tally you know we not going to answer that question," the drive said. "Don't worry."

Boy, I hated when correction officers, prison's caseworker, and as well, the administration staff told me not to worry, when I worried about weather or not I'd make parole, when I worried about making it to lower security, and when I worried about my release date. Their main saying, were not to worry. *Easy for you to say,* I kept to myself.

"Keep your eyes on the road, and you'll see your destination," the other screw chuckle, as he turned slightly in his seat to look back at us with a smirk written on his sunburned face.

"You see, you see!" 2X call out. "That's why they call them screws; you see the smirk on that sucker fried face?" We all laugh and begin telling different jokes about why we thought convicts gave correction officers the name screw.

"You guys should better get off that issue," the driver interrupted, "or I'll write reports on all six of you. You guys in enough trouble."

"Come on man we just laughing to keep from crying," Jesse Managult who sat at the right of me, said.

By the time, those words rolled off the tongue of my friend, the van had turned into the parking lot at Walpole maximum-security prison. Norfolk was only a rock throw away from Walpole. In fact, because while Walpole with its white painted walls and white painted buildings set in a small glade, Norfolk prison sat on a small hill, making it possible for prisoners at Norfolk to look down upon Walpole's seclusion.

TEN

DEPARTMENT of SEGREGATION UNIT BLOCK 10

When I leaned my torsos over the shoulders of 2X's and glimpsed through the grated window after the van had stopped, in the rear of the prison, the first thing I noticed was what looked like chin-linked dog kennels. However, I knew from the many stories told by prisoners that they were convicts exercise cages used by isolated prisoners housed in the DSU, or "Department of Segregated Unit," better known as "ten block."

"Hay screw," 2X roared; "why we not going through the front door!"

"Because you bad boys gone to ten block, he replied, as he opened the van's rear doors.

"Woooo, ten-block, they got some real shit heads inside there," spoke the other screw standing next to his buddy.

One-by-one we stepped from the van into the sultry August day, where a hand full of ten-block's screws, with grin on their face, awaited us near the steel doors that lead to ten-block.

"Thanks boys we got them now," burked the sergeant in the pack, wearing a crew cut hair style with the side of his head shaved almost bald.

As ten-block officers escorted us into ten-block, again I felt that mixed feeling of both fear and courage. Fear that anything might happen to me in ten. Nevertheless, my courage assured me that I'd be okay. Ten block was vulgar, unpredictable, loud, and psychotic. Cons were forever and a day in conflict with themselves and with the administration, about one thing or another.

The administrators at Walpole already had a whole block, on the first floor, in the notorious ten-block sat aside to receive us. Each cellblock or "row" had fourteen cells, twelve barred cells and two solid steel doors used for complete isolation.

Moreover, except for the corroding toilets, in each our cells, the cells had been lately cleaned and only just painted a royal blue with the fresh odor of lead paint hanging heavily in the air. However, though the odor of the painting strong, it did give the block a fresh scent. It seemed as though the administration had done its job. It had reckoned ahead of time and had gotten the ten- block, or the "row" ready for us, "Norfolk ring leaders." Why had they painted?

Well, our guess was that the warden had figured that since we had gotten so much new coverage and support from the outside world, that once we arrived at ten-block, we's surly get visitors from members of the state legislators trying to find out what sparked the work stoppage, why the lugging, and had we been abused. If that was the warden's plan, he was right because we did get visits from both members of the Senate and the House of Repersentive.

By the time the screws took the irons off our wrists and ankle, and stripped us, there were twelve of us on the row from Norfolk. They placed me in cell one nearest the shower and front of the block. Paul Little was placed next to me in cell two while Tom Swift, a jail house lawyer, also serving life with without parole in cell three. Tally and Jesse Managult ... were in the center ... and 2X at the far end near the two steel doors, the "burial chambers." Back at Concord, years ago, I'd done fifteen-days in a similar, isolation cell for being drunk off vanilla extract.

After we had made our bunk, and had settled in the best we could under our living conditions, a meeting was called be no other than 2X and seconded by Managult to discuss our living plan. The twelve decided we need a chairperson and after discussing it for a few minutes, they undividedly choose me as their chairperson. I immediate suggested we go on a hunger strike, and would remain so until the system, the central office in Boston, return us to Norfolk. For no administration but central office could approve our return, they were now calling all the shots on us.

The group agreed to drink only water, coffee, and tea. However, since I practiced yoga and fasted regularly, I knew from prior experience that caffeine wasn't at all good for a body fasting because it made the person quivery; as if having a diabetes attack. Nevertheless, I was the only one who chooses to drink only water. The rest of the group decided to drink their coffee and tea, as well.

We also elected a legal advisor, and that responsibility went to Tom Swift. In addition, since we were stuck in ten-block for who knows how long, we should make ourselves as comfortable as possible. Therefore, since Tally had the Harlem drug connection through his wife, we elected him, the dope "Man." Thus, every Thursday, without fail, Tally's wonderful wife flew into Boston from Harlem to visit her Tally; and every Thursday Tally came through.

Hell, the screws knew we were getting high and knew that Tally's wife was bringing in the dope. Not only were we getting drugs on the row, but also at times, the guards would open the steel lock doors, which separated visit from prisoner, and let Tally sex it up with his wonderful wife. Well that's what Tally told us. Ten-block, like Walpole, was one big drug den. The screws knew that if prisoners were getting high, we were less of a problem, making their jobs a whole lot easier.

The screws also knew when there weren't any drugs in the cellblocks, because the whole place turned into an asylum. It were on those days that we twelve went at each other throat, from the sheer boredom of being locked down in a cage twenty-three hours a day— most times, twenty-four hours a day, without TV or radio. We got to the point where we challenged each other with threats of harm if ever the moments allow it. However, because of the schedule of ten-block's lock down, it was unlikely anyone make real his threats. For two convicts were never supposed to be out of their cells together; nevertheless, in ten-block anything could happen.

Ten-block reminded me of a novel I once read, *No Exit,* by Paul Sartre. We too, got on each other nerves similar to the three characters in the novel, which had died and sent to hell, a small room painted all white to live the rest of their lived. We threaten to punch each other's lights out whenever we went outdoors to exercise. However, knowing full well, that if we were lucky enough to get an hour of exercise and fresh air we'd be put in separate dog lookalike kennels. We went out for exercises so infrequently that by the time we did, we were boys again and all threats were off, leaving us to enjoy the sun and birds and the splendid blue sky.

There was one thing we never done; we never throw anything out of our cells at the screws. Tom Swift had a habit cursing at them, however, most screws just let his insults roll of their shoulders. The ones who felt insulted were the ones most likely to spice his food with cough ups, urine, household cleanser ...

When our property finally arrived from Norfolk, the only and most important items missing were our televisions and radios sets. From fear of watching the news and seeing how successfully the strike was going, the system denied to give them to us. Therefore, the only information we received came from other convicts housed in ten-block, other three cellblocks. They'd yell from their cells whenever the news came on letting us know that the strikers were unyielding and that the people from the street were still outside the wall showing their support. For that kind of news it was worth being in, ten-block.

Norfolk prisoners were holding strong and demanding that the system return the twenty-seven prisoners lugged. They demonstrated one afternoon by standing in the two prison years and on the quad, in pouring rain, for twenty-seven minutes—a minute for each prisoner lugged. By that time the twenty-seven of us became know to the media as, "Norfolk Twenty-seven."

Some of the other fifteen prisoners lugged ended up in the dusky, muggy, and covered with goo dungeon on "Beacon Street" at Bridgewater State Prison, built in the nineteenth century. Beacon Street was an area at Bridgewater where the visiting room, chapel, inmate vocation, law library, and library where. Moreover, beneath the buildings loomed the dungeon. Why was that area called Beacon Street was unknown to prisoners at that time.

In addition, the other prisoners lugged ended up in block-9, or Department of Segregated Unit, at Concord. A best friend, Annie King, kept us, via mail, informed on their living condition in the dungeon, which he described as "Gothic evil"; and another friend, Greg Davis, kept us on par about their quandary at Concord. Everyday, we wrote back-and-forth to each other; letter written so clearly that it seemed as if we were experiencing one another condition.

The dungeon hadn't been used or opened for some twenty plus years because it was unfit for human utilization. The courts had long condemned it. However, the system had only one thing in mind—gaining back the control of its prison at Norfolk. Moreover, if that meant sticking ringleaders and troublemakers in a filthy, wet, gummy, spider webbed, and condemned pit, so be it.

However, as the row's chair I realized after nine days, without food that I had a decision to make. I realized that the Massachusetts Department of Correction had no intention, of returning Norfolk Twenty Seven back to Norfolk. For to do so, would be a slap in the fact; and they were not going to give in to a bunch of troublemakers, as they depicted us. I also was willing to bet a small wedge that my eleven comrades felt the same way. Nevertheless, ten- block had hardened them, and they were trying so desperately to stick to the hunger strike and be unbreakable. Tom Swift would have hungered to his death, and said so. Tom wasn't really all there, and reminded me of a cave hermit; bony with long red hair and a long red beard. Nevertheless, he got along well with other prisoners—most jailhouse lawyers did. Tom was a cool dude, though.

The next morning, when I thought all my comrades were awake, I called a morning meeting to convey that we should consider breaking the hunger strike, and wasn't surprised when all eleven voiced, "stick to the strike." I really admired their show of strength; however, if we continued on our present mission, we would soon self-destruct and still not end up back at Norfolk. It would only be a waste of time to go on.

Yes, the prisoners at Norfolk were sticking to their guns. The peaceful work stoppage was fully charge. Yet, I still felt that we weren't going back. For that would give us too much influence over the other prisoners. Thus, as chairperson I made the decision that we'd break our hunger strike at the noon meal. Everyone boasted that they'd not eat until they were return to Norfolk. Therefore, when the screws came by with the noontime meal tray, they first stopped at my cell.

"You guys eating today," the screw carrying one of the meal trays jokingly asked.

"Give me a tray," I announced loudly enough for all to hear, "I'm hungry." The screws were in shock when they heard my announcement, for I had caught them completely off guard.

"You serious, Elow?"

"Give me a tray."

The freckles face screw pouring the tea, stopped in his tracks, laughed and said, "It's about damn time you're eating because you not going back Norfolk. You guy f... sick!" Everyone took a tray except for, my main man, Jesse Managult. Jesse, his brother Ernie, and I, were tighter than some brothers were. The two were both hustles and pocket-pickers.

Yeah, but when the supper tray came around, Jesse took a tray of food and before he could sat down at his small metal table, which sat at the foot of his bunk, to dig into his food after ten-days without, we were all over him in play—for eating.

"I just know managult not eating," Paul Little teased.

"Hay Paul," Tally bellowed. "He got that food for me. Ain't that right, Jess?"

"Come on now, y'all," I said in Jesse's defense. "Leave the brother along and stop blocking me out. Y'all know he got the tray for me. That's my food."

"Hay Jesse," 2X cracked. "F... them dudes, man; I give you a joint for it."

We played and teased back-and-forth while we all enjoyed our supper. I couldn't see the faces of the cons on the row, yet I felt that we were all delighted that Jesse had eaten. By eating our bodies, built strength and our mind and spirit were more in hominy with the twelve of us. Thus, we were not as cranky and threatening—towards each other—as we were before eating. The strike lasted three-months; and it's said that our peaceful work stoppage, strike, inside a prison's wall, was the longest peaceful work stoppage on prison record.

Well, we'd done our best, in a peaceful way, to protect our family and friends from the humiliation of being skinned-search. Moreover, because of our deficit the administration, under superintendent, Michael V. Fair, went right on stripping and humiliating our kin and friends.

Days after the strike ended, one-by-one, D. O. C. begun classifying us out of ten-block to their other state prison in the system, excluding Norfolk. Tally, the Man, because he only had fifteen days to wrap up his five-years and a day sentence they transferred him to minimum security at Concord Farm. Can't say that he made out on that deal, for if he had not been in ten, he would have already been at Boston Pre-release Center. Nevertheless, he made out better in his transfer, than the rest of us.

Because the D. O. C. had it in for Jesse Managult and me, 2X McDonald, Paul Little and Tom Swift, and called ringleaders with too much influence over other prisoners, we were classified to remain at Walpole, but in its population. To transfer us from ten-block into Walpole's population, we need not go outdoors into the pleasurable autumn weather, which would have been cool. However, I can remember that late morning when I left ten-block.

Tally was the first one in ten to get his move; then, a few days later I was escorted out of ten-block by officer Gilbow, who was one of the fairest correction officers at Walpole. He was, about 5-5, with a blond curly afro, which he wore well, for a white dude. Big Moose, the other screw escorting me was big and brawny. Hell, the guy's hand were twice the side of mines put together.

While we shot the shit with each other on the row, we heard that all too familiar ringing of keys, then, the squeaking of the heavy barred gate being unlock and push forward.

"Okay! Elow," Big Moose uttered. "It's time to go." We on the row liked Big Moose, for he respected you if you respected him. Like I said Moose was a big fellow, and if need be, he had no problem taking a prisoner down, even with force.

"Yeah," Gilbow said, teasing the guys left on the row." Later Elow goanna be walking the big yard with his boys, Roger West and Johnny Stephanie, who run Walpole with drugs—"

"He better be cool out there, 2X warned. "They don't play out there."

Big Moose unlocked my cell door and gave me one of those screws' grins, and announced out of the clear blue sky, "Yeah, Tally was the big man in here, huh." His statement took us by surprise. I guess we were all thinking if they knew so much, why hadn't they bust Tally and his wife? "Come on cut the shit. Did you guys think you got over on us?" Big Moose went on while Gilbow locked the cuff around my wrists. "We knew what you guys were up to from the beginning. We know Tally was the big man on the row and you guys were high most days of the week."

"Man!" Jesse exclaimed. "Ain't nobody the man."

"Say good-by to your friend," Gilbow said as he firmly wrapped his hand around my right upper arm.

92

"Man get out of here!" the boys left behind shouted. Most prisoners had a low moment watching other prisoners leave them. Yet some could careless.

All the way to the robust solid steel door, with only a round hole in its center, the size of a mayo cap, Big Moose kept talking about Tally being the man on the row.

At the steel door, leading into Walpole, Gilbow unlocked and opened a small black box, attached to the wall, and made a phone call from the phone within. Just then, Big Moose unlocked to door and the three of us stepped into a small holding cell. When Big Moose had locked the door behind us, a door similar to the one we had just gone through, opened on the Walpole side. Gilbow and Big Moose passed me over to, two young sprucely Walpole screws, looking as though they'd just gotten out of D. C. O. cadet school. The whole transfer seemed as though I'm being traded off to another country. The two young guards and I entered Walpole population, and again I walked down the same corridor I'd walked down, as a new man when first arriving at Walpole some eighteen-months ago.

Because Tally Davis only had a few weeks to wrap up his five years and a day sentence—sixty months and one day—he was send across the street to Concord Farm; a minimum-security facility, to milk cows at 4:30 a. m. Yes, milking cows at 4:30 in the morning beat being stuck in ten-block. However, Tom Swift, though highly educated, with a degree in Clinical Psychology, wasn't too bright when it came time to say, enough. He refused to see the classification board, and made a written request to remain in ten-block.

However, who can say why some prisoners would rather live lock down in a vindictive environment. Sometimes, twenty-four hours a day, in a psychotic setting, with the air and sky opened to them.

Just walking the big yard was a God given consecration. Yet there were prisoners, like Tom, who thrive in that type of manure. It gave them, I believe, a sense of empowerment to take their behavior out on both screws and cons. Some cons never learn that, "you can't beat the system."

ELEVEN

CHICKEN and the High NOON WARRIORS

On one of those bright and sunny, Sunday mornings, some few months into population, Johnny Stephan, a friend of mines strong, tall loudmouthed, athletically lean with the built of a Spartan and skin as black and shiny as a mirror, walked into A-3 in the minimum-security end where I housed. He then strolled to the back of the block where Jerry Funderburg also serving life without parole, Weasel and I were hanging out after sharing a bag of heroin and smoked a joint.

"Man!" Johnny bellowed, turning to see if the screw sitting at his desk at the far end of the flat near the opened barred gate was watching him. The screw pretended not to notice him or us as he read one of Boston's daily newspapers. "Man!" Roger just got stab by a white boy in A-1!" Jonny and Roger West were rock solid friends and co-defenders, and each serving twenty-years for a bank sting. In addition, they were partners in the prison's drug dealings and hooch—or makeshift wine making.

"What!" Jerry erupted, as he stops picking his Gil Scott Herson style, afro. Then poking and squeezing his mouth forward as if it were a suction cup, troublesomely growl, "Man! Who the punk that did it?"

"Why did he get stabbed?" Weasel asked revengefully, wiggling his fingers at his side.

"Does the white boy have jailhouse support—"

"The white dude," Johnny fumed, cutting me off, "owed us for some pills we sold him three weeks ago. We began charging him interest on everyday he didn't pay, and, his bill kept gone up. He promised to pay up last night, after his visiting hour. Roger went to collect the money this morning, and the guy didn't have the money. So Roger stepped into the dude cell, unplugged his color TV set and his fan, for pay. But out of nowhere the sucker, shank him." I had to remind Johnny to keep his voice down.

"Yeah, he got two brothers in here and a few boys. But I don't give a f… about his brothers or his boys," Johnny barked. "But thank God, Roger seen the shank coming and side stepped it, catching it in his right side instead of his spine. The wound is a small one. He didn't even need go to the hospital."

"What we goanna do about it?" Jerry asked, as he stopped picking his large afro and stuck the black pick into his bushy hair. Jerry, like most us was a street fighter and loved a good fight as much as he loved getting high. He was one of my closes friends—we were boys to the bone.

"We goanna to T. C. B.," Weasel said, wiggled his fingers at his side.

As we plotted, Roger West came striding down the flat toward us likes a John Wayne—proud, handsome, and as tall as six five. Moreover, because of his great ability to play basketball, he forever looked as if he were ready for a rebound. We all stopped talking when he approached, *Hell he looks fine to me,* I thought.

Johnny broke the salient, "We can't let that white dude get away with that. Man, if we do our reputation in the whole system will be suspect. F… that!"

"That punk tried to kill me or something," Roger heatedly uttered, looking around to see if he was overheard.

There were other cons chatting on the flat and the two tiers above us; but no one gave us any thought. However, by now, the three housing blocks in minimum- security were blaring with noise as one big market place; where cons gathered for funs and games … , shooting pool, playing cards and ping pong; purchasing marijuana, pills, dope, LSD, or self-made booze.

Since we were standing near Bow Burns' opened cell, a friend of ours, who was out getting high, I suggested we talk in his cell. I'm sure he wouldn't have minded. Nevertheless, even if he had, he'd say nothing at a time like this. However, any other time he would have kicked us out. Any other time we would have not gone into his cell at all, if he wasn't in it. Bow was far from lacking courage. As we talked, Jerry stood at the door's entrance as the look out.

"We goanna need a crew, "Weasel weaseled.

"We need to be at lease six deep," Roger said.

"I'm down!" I enthusiastically volunteered. I hadn't been in a pack rumble since my gang days when I was still a teenager. Moreover, sometimes a good fight was a good way of releasing prison's tension and depression.

"No!" Johnny barked. "No way, you stick to politics and let us handle this. Plus, you know my father. Blue would cuss me out if something happen to you." We all laughed.

"Okay man, I hear you. Keep your voice down." Blue, a nickname, was Johnny's father and a friend of mines who had toured the same dice games out there in the street, which I had. We thought each other humorous and thus became friends. Blue was as loud as his son.

Roger lit a couple joints and passed one to me, as he poked on the other. I took a few pulls and passed it to Jerry while Roger passed his own as well …

With those words coming from Johnny's mouth, I did't say another word in the assistant of their plans. The son of a, friend of mines, was telling me to continue using my brain to fight.

The plot was in play, Johnny and Roger would first go over block A-2 and meet with some of the white leaders to see if they'd reason with the young man to pay his balance due, and avoid a war.

The white leaders told Johnny and Roger when they met that the "kid" didn't have any money to pay his debt; furthermore, he would not give up his television or any of his personal property to them. In other words, the white leaders told them to get lost. Thus, the war was on; and the two parties agreed that since it was Sunday and they'd be bake chicken served for lunch, they'd use that time to solve their differences.

Hence, since they only served each prisoner a half bake chicken once a month, everyone would go to lunch, leaving the three-blocks empty of cons and screws, which would give the fighters ample time to get their battle on. They also agreed that each party would have no more that six fighters, just as Roger had stated early. The weapons used would be whatever they got their hands on.

When Johnny and Roger returned to block A-3, they called their crew together to explain what the deal was. At noon, with the aroma of bake chicken dominating the air in the corridor, and seeping into the blocks, the guards in inner control announced over the intercom, "Chow time, chow time!"

With the announcement made all three minimum-security blocks inmates from: A-1, A-2, and A-3 rowdily filed out of their cells and blocks into the well-lighted, high polished corridor bound for the mess hall, which sat at the halfway point, between the minimum-security end and the maximum-security end and across from inner-control. However, the two duel combatant groups remained behind ready for a showdown.

Weasel and I stood in A-3, directly across from the battler zone. I was surprise to see Weasel standing at my side, for I thought he was down with the fracas. Nevertheless, I nudged him with my left elbow when I saw the white combatants all carrying table legs; they'd stripped from the oak tables in the game rooms, descending the front stairwell in A-2 and lining themselves width the flat.

"Damn," Weasel whispered; "they already got the advantage with-with them table legs."

Cool Weasel had some way weaseled his way out the fight. Hell, I told you the man was smooth. I again nudged him with my elbow when I saw the brothers emerging from beneath the back stairwell, at the other of the block and lined themselves width the flat.

Slowly, and similar to gladiatorial they advanced toward each other and clashed, striking each other with oak table legs, hammers, shanks, and lead pipes. I could see Roger, towering above all the other, as his long bronzed colored arm swung his hammer at the Iron Man's head. Iron Man Hercules built from years of lifting weight, moved his head just in time, which caused the hammer to strike him between the shoulders blade and neck. The blow caused Iron Man to drop his table lag and fall against the steel wall.

Roger tried with the quickness to finish him off; however, one of Iron Man's boys stepped in and caught Roger just blow his right hip, near his stab wound, with such a blow that I closed my eyes expecting to feel his pain. The young baby-face Irishman who had struck him rushed at him. However, Roger swung his hammer and struck him below the right eye. The Irishman stumbled and fell to his knees bleeding ferociously.

Roger turned his attention back to the Iron Man, who'd gain some composure. Consequently, by now with both men wounded they fought like drunks. I looked and saw one of those four-corners oak legs bounce off Jerry's head.

"Damn!" Weasel frowned, his lean body quivering from head to shoe. "That hurt! Shit! The man is hurting. He better not go down."

"I hope all that afro he's got softens the blow," I said as we continued watching and judging the competition.

Jerry also knew that he had better not go down, for that would be the end of him. Therefore, he managed to stick his attacker in the upper thigh with an ice pick shaped shank, which he had tapped to his right hand. The attacker short, stocky and very bald, limped one-step backward, however, quickly regained his senses and rushed at Jerry swinging his table leg wildly; hitting one of the steel walls, which sent a thunderous noise throughout the cellblocks.

"I just know somebody heard that," Weasel grumbled; then, frowns as if someone had stepped on his toes.

Johnny was bleeding from his head, with blood dripping from his right chin onto his shoulder; staining his white T. shirt, with the pattern of crimson. In addition, the other brothers, hurt and energy spent; couldn't get pass the table legs. So at that point, they had two choices, fight of flight. Choosing the latter, they barricaded themselves in one of the cells. If they hadn't, the brothers would have been Bloody Maris.

All six managed to pile into the bathroom size cell and held the door shut while the triumphant combatants tried pulling it open; however, the retreaters dared not let go of the door. The thunderous noise from the table leg smashing into the steel wall brought the screws flying out of the mess hall into the corridor. Some of them moved swiftly toward the minimum end while others quickly locked down the mess hall, securing the chicken eating, cons within.

By now, A-2 was swarming with screws, and the white boys, like junkyard dogs forming at the mouths were still trying, with their hands to pry open the cell door—that housed the defeated. When the screws ordered the victors to put down their weapons and go into the game room. There was no resistant. Hell, why should they resist, when they'd won the battle.

A group of screws escorted both parties back to their cells, and another group of screws took Johnny, Iron Man, Roger, and Jerry to the prison's infirmary, for treatment. Therefore, except for a few stitches here and there, and a few heads bandaged, according to the prison's doctor, no one was seriously injured. With their medical examination done and each given a prescription for Tylorine, the screws took each con back to his cell to wait a lugging to ten-block. Later that afternoon all twelve rivals were then rounded up and take either to ten-block or to maximum-security—block-2.

I felt offended to witness the brothers, not only getting their asses kicked, but to retreat, also, that I wanted to find a mouse hold to hide. Nevertheless, on that day, I learnt an important lesson: If your're going to war you damn well better be prepared for it.

By now, the entire prison was on lock down and cons didn't leave their cells again for recreation until supper time and after the 5:30 p.m. count. It was as though nothing had happen during the high noon lunch. The cons in minimum were as busy as the "bird of action," or the hummer bird, and noisy as a shipyard. Cons were in and out of each other cells getting high while others at the gymnasium either played basketball or worked their bodies, lifting iron.

Walpole was a vicious and chaotic place, and difficult for any prisoners who wanted to cultivate his life to do so. I hadn't done much with my life the whole time I spent there; and did what at least eight-five percent of other prisoners did, I got high. However, heroin and cocaine played its part in the prison's drug trade, marijuana and "Tylorine," a small orange pill with and opium effect that could be either snorted or injected played the major roles.

In 1973, four years before my going to Walpole, the prison's doctors were dispensing Tylorine and Benadryl to prisoners like candy. Who ever complained to having anxiety or a mental disorder the "jailhouse doctors" gave them Tylorine, and who ever complained of sleepless nights given Benadryl. Mixing the Benadryl together with the Tylorine prevented headaches, the side effect Tylorine. The two drugs mixed together gave off a high similar to heroin. Walpole also had its aspirins and Tylenol poppers. Hell, everyone in the joint seemed stressed out, including the screws. Nevertheless, the beat went own without skipping a day.

When the jailhouse doctors finally stopped dispensing the small orange pills to prisoners, around the early 1973 it caused the prisoners to riot, which set off the "pill riot." With cons taking over some control of the prison's interior—the screws scrambling for the out of control trap doors and exit themselves out into the parking lot until further notice.

Some weeks later, after convicts had tired themselves down from drugging and partying—Walpole's screws alone with the state troopers managed to enter the prison's interior cracking heads until they had again regained government power. In this, riot the state troopers did enter the institution, and didn't leave until they'd turned the joint back over to Centurial Office.

Walpole had been in a clutter, before the state troopers took it back, and everything from Scotch to a myriad of drugs floated through the big corridor and cellblocks on either end of security during the "pill riot." You see, the administration didn't cut off cons visits. Moreover, women visitors boldly made their way into sections of the cellblocks, lugging with them their sexism, dope and booze. Thus, there were an abounded of get high circling the Big House. Cons thought that they were in the street. Because if they need dope in the middle of the night, they would leave their unlock cell, walk a few feet, knock on the pusher's door and served.

Many of the locks on the cell doors were broken; toilets and sinks ripped from their walls and water rolled off the tiers onto the flats. Trash, burnt blankets, smoking mattresses, and soiled water sent out a gassy charred odor. The pharmacy raided for its drugs, and the kitchen and mess hall damaged, leaving the cons to live in their destruction and glum for months, before the administration fixed and made repairs to the interior of the prison.

After the "pill riot," Walpole didn't changed much. Prisoners were still getting high; and for at least a year, they murdered each other monthly for a dope deal gone badly, for not paying a bill, for loss of a sport event, for a loss card game, for stitching ... , and sometimes for jealousy.

I knew that my nonconformist behavior had to stop if I wanted to get out of the Walpole. Thus, I decided to slow down so that I might make a minimum-security transfer out of Walpole. In fact, I'd remained drug free for thirty days in order to learn how to practice TM, Transcendental Meditation from the Maharish Maha Yogi classes, sponsored by Harvard University. The prison officials had offered TM to prisoners who were interest in the class, hoping it would relieve the inmates' tension, stress, and anxiety; and teach them how to relax. The administration figured that if it could get the hardcore cons to enter the TM program perhaps, then, they would become better persons.

At first, from fear of losing their respect or life, the tough guys couldn't see themselves ever, in TM classes with their eyes closed and furthermore, to them, TM was a sucker's thing.

Well, drip-by-drip, some of the tough guys begun signing up for TM. The program caught fire and successfully spread from Walpole into Massachusetts other state prisons. A year or so later with some help coming from TM and other occupational programs the prison had begun, like: music, art, education, outside discussion groups … , the murder rate dropped at Walpole and not long after changing its name to Cedar Junction they stopped … However, don't get me wrong, the prison is still a level, five.

Well, for me, for years now, I'd been practicing Hatha Yoga, some mischief meditation, and reading books on eastern philosophy and the myriads of religious books that I could place my hands on in quest for self reconciliation: to cleanse my body, mind, and soul from its constant impurities.

To this point, I was a cradle Roman Catholic and rear in a Catholic home. However, in the 1960s the Church and Vatican were going through changes and adjustments, and so was my life. Consequently, I drifted away from the Church in quest of finding that hope and peace the Church so broadly professed in the name of, Jesus Christ. Not only did I, search and study philosophy and other religions for that calmness; but also thought that I might find that peace, even in drugging.

TWELVE

CAMP WARRICK

In February 1980, I did transfer from Walpole to minimum-security. Walpole shipped me out to Warrick Forestry Camp, way up there in Orange, Massachusetts on the Mohawk Trail, between the Quabbin Reservoir and the New Hampshire border. There I worked as building janitor, which gave me, the opportunity to be inquisitive and all over the place. I quickly built a trust between the officers, the administration, and me by being a hard worker and my own man. I'd the privilege of going places alone, where other inmates couldn't go. If I wanted to get away for a while to read and relax, I take to the visiting room between visits.

I also had been taking a course in creative writing where our writer instructor taught me and other inmates the craft of dialogue, leaving narration to our natural instincts and experiences. With a wonderful writer instructor guiding us, I did sit down to writing a novel: *Guns to Freedom,* a novel where three fierce black gunmen who took it upon themselves to become abolitionists. The theme is a fast gun western. The novel is still sitting in the morgue with my many other stories.

What a graceful thing to have left the barbaric, blaring, and vile condition at Walpole. The camp—built in the middle of the forest surround by majestic pine trees, with one road in and out. The buildings, themselves, all built of clapboards stained brown from weather, element, and time: The main cabin with two wings dormitories, kitchen, visiting room, office space, and guardroom, was clean, low key, and welcoming. The officers wore civilian clothes and respectfully treated the inmates.

I took pleasure in the bitter cold winter at Warrick. The snow flaks, the size of quarters falling to the ground in fluffs, with wind wailing in the trees. Additionally, on a clear full moon night, it seemed as though the moon was three time its normal size, lighting up the forest that would ordinarily be black. To look up at the stars so bright and sparkling, and so near to earth, gave me a strange and infinite feeling.

The camp was *joie de vivre* and peaceful. At night after supper, when the kitchen workers had finished their work and everyone out of the dining room, I would pick up my yellow pad and pencils from my desk, where I shared a cubical with another inmate and head to the dining room to work on my novel in peace.

In September of that same year, I made a move to Boston Pre-release Center in Dorchester. If I thought Warrick cordial, then Boston Pre-release was almost like home. While there, I got a job in the Boston garment district, and had the privilege of frequently visiting with family while on furloughs.

However, again, just that quick the street was already getting hold of my life. Honestly, I no longer had an interest in marriage life. Marcia would be much better off with her lover, for I knew that for years Marcia was having an affair with a married man with children. I further knew that at first, she did it for his support, so that she could feed and dress the children and pay the bills. She really pumped him for years. For when I was away, the yellow-skinned country and homey looking lover took *real* good care of her and the children. However, each time I got out Marcia and I picked up where we'd left off, husband and wife. Nevertheless, she did go out with her sugar daddy each, and every Friday night. She called it her night out. I never did let on to her, that I'd once seen her, through our living room window, get out of his run down station wagon, at 4:00 a.m. on a Saturday morning.

I really din't care about her sugar daddy, fruiting off on Friday night with her; she really needed a better man than myself taking care of her. However, she was still my wife and I knew that she still love me. All I need to do was let go of heroin and mature, and we'd live that wonderful vow of marriage. I so badly wanted to be a good husband and father. I had four wonderful beautiful healthy children and a wife who remain at my side for twenty-four years—and perhaps suffered the blows of my stupidity more than I had.

Anyway, once at Boston Pre-release I hooked up again with Pamela Brighton, a graduate of Wellesley College whom I had met at Bridgewater State Prison when I was there for a short time. Pam would come into BX-Bridgewater minimum-security section to work on an improvisational play. Thus, I put on my theater masks and audition for the head character position in the play.

Everyone in the play, some five or six troupe, and director Pam, all had a part in both producing, directing and improvising the play; there was no script. First, we needed a name; and after brainstorming with this and that name for some crazy reason we named the play, *The Life Story of Dave Turkey*. In the play, I played the young seventeen-year-old Dave Turkey, though I a mustache and was thirty-four at the time.

The Life Story of Dave Turkey was of a young man from Springfield, Massachusetts who had gotten himself busted, for armed robbery and sentenced to Walpole to serve 3 – 5 years. Later on in his sentence, the guards found him in his cell murdered by another prisoner, whose cell Dave had broken into stealing the inmate's electric fan to buy prison's drugs.

Pam was a natural sandy blonde, short, sexes, appetizing, and sported a tight lean runner's body. Moreover, not only did she process a well-cultured brain; she was also hip, and no smooth talking prisoner could play her. She knew in her decency not to feed in to prisoners' wishes. Pam was very sensitive to the needs of people, but no fool. However, every time she came into the prison, my body flamed, while fluid and thoughts awaited my night.

When I arrived at Boston Pre-release Center, Pam lived in JP—or Jamaica Plain, right down the road from the center, less than a mile away. It took my five minutes to reach her house driving my BMW. Therefore, I spent a great deal of time at her house. We often sat on her back porch after our workdays, having a wine and cheese snacks while taking pleasure in the summer braze. Nevertheless, I never made love to Pam, not even when it was wide open to me.

For there was that one Friday night when out spending a weekend furlough at home with my family, and Pam's roommate, Patty Morgan, being out of town, Pam invited me over to her place for dinner, where we then ate by candle. With Pam, being from rural Connecticut and Patty being from rural New Hampshire and both from the hippy's culture, their apartment wore a pastoral décor and was very neat. The table we dined at was a huge wooden country table; partially covered, at its center, with a tan neutral, textural weave tablecloth. On top of the tablecloth, in tall wooden candle holders were two-lit candle, and between them sat an old strew basket, filled with dried white roses.

After eating, Pam invited me into her bedroom to look at her family photo album. Once in the room I wanted so much to take her into my arms. However, I didn't want to seem, to her, that all I wanted was that cute little body. Nevertheless, we left her room and went into the living room where we talked tell 1:00 p.m. before I announced my departure Pam invited me again into her bedroom to look at the same family photo album.

I wanted her so dreadfully that it hurt. Moreover, here she was all for the taking and still, I did not take her. Why hadn't I taken her into my arms, brought her over and laid her down on her big fluffy, country-style made bed? On the other hand, was I perhaps telling her that sex wasn't everything; and I could past it up for friendship instead. For here we stood, our bodies almost touching and I did not bind my lips to her waiting mouth.

About six month into my stay at the Boston Pre-release Center, Pam and I were having one of our wine and cheese snacks on her back porch after a day of work. Pam at that time was still working in the prison system and I worked, in China Town, for the textile, "Lady in Waiting" shipping and receiving.

It was late August, and as a light wind breezed through the foliages that surrounded Pam's house; she and I enjoyed our snacks while tall trees reaching out to the blue heaven were everywhere. In fact, Pam lived one-half-block away from Franklin Park—one of eight parks, or "emeralds" designed by Fredrick Law Olmsted.

As we snacked, Pam declared, "I'm in love!" I thought I heard and understood her; however, I wasn't too sure. Therefore, I asked her, what she'd said. "I'm in love! Elow, I'm in love."

I truly believed that Pam throw that fastball at me to test my reaction. Well, if that was her intention it worked. Because my left hand in which I held a piece of cheese stopped in mid air on its way to my mouth. *She's in love with me!* I thought.

"You're in love?" I confirmed, thinking Williams Shakespeare to myself. *"And make my seated heart knock at my ribs."*

"Yes, I'm in love," she said, looking at me with a slight grin moving across her mouth, which led me to believe that she was also playing games with my head; getting back at me for not making love to her that night. "Ah huh, I'm in love with Scott."

My mouth slightly opened closed tightly and my left hand holding the cheese rested on the table while the other hand reached for the stem less wine glass, which held the fruity red wine and we toasted to her joy of love, "Ting."

"How long have you been in love with Scott?" I discreetly asked her reaching across the table for a finger sandwich while wishing her, a sincerely long and happy life with Scott.

I'd met Scott more than a few times at Pam's. I can say that we were friends. Nevertheless, I never picked up any vibes between him and Pam. I never noticed any warmth coming from them either. However, right after she told me how she felt about Scott, it was then that they began romancing in public.

With Scott and Pam hooked up, Pam's friend and roommate, and a graduate of Wellesley College, Patty Morgan, made her move to engage me in a relationship. I believe that Patty wanted to be with me since we'd first met sometime ago, when she came to our play, *The Life Story of Dave Turkey* at Bridgewater. However, she held back because she really thought that Pam and I had a thing going. Therefore, now that Pam had her man, Patty began audaciously flirting with me.

There were times when I'd caught Patty glancing at me whenever I visited Pam and now Scott. On occasions she would sit across from me when we ate out on the porch together, with her legs opened enough for me to see her flowering shrub. Once when I'd passed her in the kitchen on my way to the bathroom, she purposely bumped in to me and our lips touched.

Thus, I warned her, "You better watch what you're doing you may not be able to handle what you're bucking for," and I would continued my way to the bathroom.

One night after one of my Transcendental Meditation sittings, I called Pam from a pay phone, on Concord Street, in Cambridge and asked her did

Patty have an appeal for me. Pam confirmed my curiosity. Then, suggest that I call Patty and ask her myself. That was exactly what I did.

Patty Morgan was a few years older than Pam, around thirty-three and stood about five four, with hair more pepper than salt. She was a country girl from New Hampshire, and at times still disclosed that rural appearance in her attire. Thank God, we were still in the culture-age of psychedelic. There was times when we went out, which was often, when I wished I could turn into the Invisible Man because of her attire.

Yes, she was hot, sizzling hot through and through and loved sexing it up. I could just touch her and she'd orgasm. We made blatant sex all over the place: The Arnold Arboretum, the movie houses, and in the car. We even lusted while waiting for the red light to turn green.

Moreover, after practicing TM in her tidy and rustic little bedroom room with its "flower child" décor, where both vibrant plants and sparkling crystal balls hung from her bedroom's two windows; we'd romance on a thick, comfortable foam mattress—lying on the floor as a soft yellow flam burned in a kerosene lamp sitting on a small table. However, by the time Patty and I broke up some six months later, she had nearly drained me of my manliness. In addition, for some strong reason, right to the end, Patty really believed that Pam and I had private affairs. Not true—yet I like her a lot.

Anyway—by the time of my discharge from Boston Pre-Release Center, September 1980, when I was still with Patty, Marcia and I had already separated, with me living with my sister, Laura. Marcia, Laura and the children believed that I was going through some kind of male menopause; and that as soon as I got over the itch, I'd return home. However, months after Patty and I'd split, I got hold of some money and invested it in heroin.

The money to get into the dope business came to me wrapped in newspaper. I had a hunch something good was going to happen to me that cold icicle, January day, 1981, with the temperature at twenty-five degrees. However, with the sun shinning brightly in mid sky, the win composed, the weather was quite bearable, if dressed warmly.

THIRTEEN

THE DEALERS and the USERS

I left home, around noon, and drove my BMW to the drug seen on the corner of Washington and Northampton streets. It was nearly 11:30 a.m., and already the dealers were already out there. Pickpockets had stopped by to cop, or buy their morning shot, of antifreeze, before off to do what they did best, pick peoples' pockets.

Antifreeze was, a joke, another name addicts called heroin in the winter months. Crapshooters, number runners, and pool players; along with addicts looking to cop, were going in-and-out of the Baby Tiger Boxing Gymnasium, number joint, and Poolroom, as though a subway station. Moreover, winos, looking like last night sleep, stood on the block drinking Port wine and playing the fool.

Bo Pete, who stood across the street between the 1864 Lounge and the Basin Street South, saw me park in front of Lewis Lounge, and slightly nodded his head letting me no that he was dealing. I drove the car rolling it towards him with my window pulled down.

"What's up, baby?" I said.

"I got it, my man and the shit's Ooooh sooo gooddd—damn!" Bo Pete exclaim as he broke down into the dope fiend dipped, bending forward, hands almost touching his shoes, and suddenly jerked himself back up while pulling on his nose with his thumb and index fingers, adjusted himself and utter "yeah man it—I got the shit. But I'm selling only quarters for hundred dollars."

"That's cool with me."

"I got to make a quick stop—"

"Come on with that shit, now," I complained, "Damn E, man—I'm not insane to have the shit on me. Just drive and wait for me on Lenox, by Harrison Avenue."

It took me only three or four minutes to reach Lenox … and when I got there, Bo Pete was already there waiting. As I pulled up to him, he opened the passenger door, got into the car and pulled the door shut. I slid a hundred dollar bill across the leather seat to him; and with his huge, puffed up and infected abscesses hands, took the money and gave me the quarter.

"Is this a full quarter?"

"Come on E, with that bull shit, man, you can feel the weight, man, you know it's right."

"I hope so," I said looking him in the eyes. "I don't want to come back for my money."

"Don't worry man. Hay, E, if you take me to the Rainbow," Bo Pete said, as he unfolded a hundred dollar bill packed with cocaine which scented up the car, "I'll snort some blazing coke with you."

I knew without a doubt that the coke was good. Hell, its whiff filled the car with a medicine like odor and I could already taste the coke in my mouth. Bo Pete took his short, cut down straw, placed it into the coke, and snorted the cocaine into his left nostril then the other.

He did this a couple times, and with out delay his body went stiff as if he were a mannequin.

"Damn, E, my face and brain are frozen, man!" he mumbles, and with those words, snuffled another blow into his nose and cordially passed the coke over to me, pinching his large nose with his fingers.

I in return snorted up a couple blows, and felt the coke as it freezes my mouth and throat. My head felt as though I had swallowed a cube of ice. I took one more hit and passed the coke to its rightful owner. "Excellent!" I said as I started the up BMW; then, turned onto Harrison Avenue.

"Man, you know that I got the best connection for dope in New York City and I didn't sell you no bull shit."

"I hope so man."

Heroin is like a high-priced woman, and to afford her I had to hustle for her, costing me everything; family, wife, children, home, jobs, and deposits, while it turned me into a lying junky, robbing me of my life. Once heroin got hold of me, I belong to her until my death or until I find a way out. I would either die or I'd retreat; and to retreat I would have to be occupational ready. There was no other way out. I had to be ready in ever category: Physical, mental, social, vocational, and economic. This is self-empowerment through self-help.

Nevertheless, after dropping Bo Pete off at the Rainbow, I Turned off Tremont Street onto Mass Ave, and drove the few blocks to Johnny Draton's shooting gallery, on the corner of Massachusetts and Harrison Avenue, and parked on Harrison across the street from the City Hospital, now known as the Boston Medical Center. On Mass Ave, I dashed up the stoops and taped on Johnny's window knowing that his doorbell didn't ring. A brown hand pulled back the soil curtain and a smooth shaved, brown head and face, peeked out. Noticing me, he exited his room to let me enter.

I stepped into the dusky hallway and immediate my nostrils filled with the aroma of fried fish, cooking in what smelled like old burnt grease, coming from one of the many rooms on the two floors above. Somewhere else up there, I heard a cat shill, after what seemed like someone had thrown something at it.

"That cat and dude always gone off," Johnny complained, as we entered his overheated miniature size room.

Already in the room were two alluring looking salt and pepper lesbian whom I knew, getting off near an old dresser, near the window with the soil certain. They were not only shooting up, but as well, pulling at each other tongue with their juice mouths, while their works were still stuck in the pit of their arms.

"Say baby," I broke in, "That speedball must be hot, huh?" The little root beer skinned sister with her short boyish hair cut, dyed jet black to a glazed, and paste to her scalp, looked at me while still trying to hold on to the tongue of her companion, and smiled.

The little white chick broke rank, stepped back, and smirked at me as if virtuous; then, booted the bloody speedball into her vein, "Oh, shut up Elow," she said squeezing her lips together and gave me of a big, "Muah!"

Most hookers, or women hooked on heroin rather be call anything but whores. Most believe that they are virtuous and dignified even if they are streetwalkers; and to call them whores, which they resent cut deep into their psychic. It's difficult enough being street hookers and addicts. However, for them to know that they carry the logo whore, tack onto their foreheads can be quite depressing for them. It isn't a lie that heroin will make a schoolgirl put down her books and pick up the "bag."

"Damn Johnny! It's hot as hell in here!" I exclaimed, looking toward the twin-size bed where a slick looking, well dressed brown-skinned brother, in his early thirties sat; and whom I knew not and had never seen before. Stuck into his left armpit, was a syringe now filled with both blood and dope, which he boosted back and forth into a vein? Addicts believed that the blood maneuverings, boosting blood in and out, in and out of the syringe into the vein, after injecting the dope strengthen their high. I believed this tail for the longest.

I gave Johnny two dollars for the use of the room, for I was holding my own works. Up tell now the two of us hadn't said a word to each other. However, when the tall slim brother rose from the bed, I set eyes on a .22 semi-automatic pistol that sat on the bed near where stranger had sat.

"I see you holding, huh." I said looking at the gun on the bed.

"You got to," he agreeably answered, picking up the gun and and placed it in his pocket.

Moreover, in what seemed like slow motion, he strolled over to the table where the hookers were preparing themselves to leave and began washing his works in a glass of water. It took the brother at least a minute before he finally got the syringe into the glass of water. The brother was jammed jelly tight, narcotized and his body hunched over so low, that the tip of his nose touched the tip of the water glass. Then, it took him another three minutes to wash out the works.

"Hay my brother—"

Johnny cut him off, "Oh, yeah, Elow, this Philly—"

"My name is Philly because I'm from Philly, Philadelphia," he muttered and quickly straightened out his long body, throwing out his long right hand—I took it in mine and we shook hands.

As the two hookers were walking out the small room, Philly cracked, "Ugh, why y'all, why don't you share some of you with me. You giving it all to each other and them tricks. You gotta add some of me to y'all life," said Philly pointing down at his crouch.

The white hooker, turned slightly to her right, looked at Philly with daggered eyes, stuck out her right hip, placed her tiny chin on her small shoulder—hand on hip, and said, "Honey, you're so f... up that that think you pointing at is dead. Really, you couldn't get it up if we paid you."

"Oh, b... go on, before you say something that you be sorry for," Philly uttered rocking back on his heels, while sticking his right hand down the front of his pants and under his testicles, the area, between testicles and anus, and frantically began scratching like he had crabs. "Damnnn! This shit good!" he cried.

"Who'd you copped from?" I asked.

"I copped from Bo Pete," Johnny said. "Bo Pete got the best shit out there."

"Yeah, that's who I copped from, too," I said.

After getting off, I hung around a while talking with Johnny and Philly. The three of us were jammed; however, Philly so messed up that he done all the talking. He just couldn't keep his mouth shut. Moreover, he told us that he was on the run from the Philadelphia authority for bank robbery.

Philly in his bragging of being a stick-up man—bank robber pull from his pocket a wade of cash and stated that he had more money at his cousin's apartment in Dorchester, where he'd stopped over. He went on rattling that he'd only been out of the Philadelphia's prison system a week and already he'd violated his parole. Now Johnny and I, we could see why Philly was so high. He'd just gotten out of prison.

Nevertheless, what made my antennas go up with curiosity was the mentioned of *more* money. I looked at Johnny who'd known me for years, and he read my mind.

"Say, Elow, can you drop me off at my cousin's house in Dorchester?"

"Yeah, my man, no problem; but how did you know I have a car?"

He pointed his long finger at my car keys sitting on the small table that I used to mix and cook my shot. He smiled, showing me two rows of perfectly white teeth, which complimented his slender brown face.

Philly knew nothing about Boston. He had heard in prison from pimps and hustlers that Boston was an oasis for players and hustlers. Thus, he chose Boston for his hid out. He had flown into Logan International Airport the day before, and had taken a cab to his cousin's place in Dorchester. On our way to Dorchester, he asked if I'd take him to New York City, the next day to buy some heroin. Since he had no friends here, I'd told him that new dealers didn't make it alone in Boston dealing dope. A lie; I just wanted to keep him close to me.

However, I did explain to him that if he put me down with the money and the business and shared the proceeds equally, I'd do it. Nevertheless, my motive was to beat him for all his cash. If I went to New York, I was going alone, or I was coming back alone.

"Yeah, yeah man, you know, you down we got to do this together!"

I dropped Philly off at his cousin's and went in with him—on his request, however.

The apartment was bright, clean, and spacious, with high polished hardwood floors. We entered the dining room where a dark brown, reflecting dining room table sat in the center of the floor, complimented by six cushioned-chairs. Out of the bedroom, the one nearest the kitchen came chasing after a small child in play the most delightful, charismatic and black chocolate-skinned woman who couldn't have been more than twenty-five. However, I didn't catch her name when Philly introduced us, for her air and manner had transfixed me. *She looks like she got it together!* I thought.

In his tidy bedroom, Philly opened the only closet door in the room where a single pair of slacks hanged awkwardly from a wire hanger. From the closet, he removed a navy blue gym bag from the top shelf, brought it to the dressed bed and dumped its contents upon it. The money still banded fell on the bed in stacks. With my heart clobbering against my brain, I almost vomit, but kept my cools.

"Damn baby, how much you got there?"

"Tell you the truth, Mr. Elow, I don't even know," Philly said, lifting his hands filled with money in to the air, then, watch as the green stacks fall onto the bed again. "You know, I never counted it. When I need some, I just stick my hand in the cookie jar—and Bingo."

"Yeah, I can see that," I said, thinking how to play him out of his sting.

"I told you we had enough cash to go to the City!" he said, grabbing his mouth with his hand, hoping his cousin didn't hear him. "I got to watch what I say around her because she don't know about me robbing a bank or using dope."

The next days, when I picked up Philly for our trip to Harlem, he came out the house be-bopped down the stoops to the car with a bundle wrapped in newspaper. Once in the car he placed the bundle on seat and said that before we did anything, he had to first, pick up some things at the grocery store for his cousin and return them to her.

As I pulled the BMW away from the curb, he was already talking faster than a teletype while vigorously rubbing his face, from forehead to chin with the palm of his right hand, while the other hand vigorously scratched at his genitals. Philly stopped scratching and rubbing long enough to unravel the newspaper, where hundred and fifty dollar bills came alive.

"That's ten grand rights there, and there's more in the house," he hoarsely said, as the heroin settled in his throat.

"Let's put the money in the trunk where it'll be safe," I suggested. "I got to get something out of the store, too."

"Man, Elow," Philly criticized, after we had exited the car at a small Latino store on Blue Hill Avenue. "You can't leave the ride, or car running, with the money, inside."

I had deliberately left the engine running, hoping he'd notice, however, just as I eased myself into the car, Philly entered the store, and I simply place the car in to drive and drove away. My life wasn't about street fear or fear of death. For I never expect to live another day. I always felt that I wouldn't be around for tomorrow. I was a hustle, accustom to taking chances while living fast and dangerously. It was Russian roulette. Thus, there after, I really, I didn't think much about Philly again. After seeing the money on the bed, the night before, I'd say that he still had thousands of dollars left at his cousin's. Nevertheless, I wasn't going to blow the money, in the trunk, trying to get it all. He and I never met again. He must have left Boston shortly after our acquaintance.

FOURTEEN

LIVING it up in BROOKLINE

My being hooked on heroin was as if I were deeply in love with a woman whom I knew wasn't at all good for me. My love for her was so demented, so psychological that I could not break loose. "Here I stand and cannot do otherwise," said Nietzsche. On the other hand was, it Martin Luther who first prose the quote?

A couple days after returning to Boston from New York, where I'd purchased some weight, or loose heroin from a friends of mine on 127th and Lenox Avenue. I quickly set up my dealers—Doug and Lamont—who'd be dealing for me out of their Jamaica Plain studio apartment.

Doug was one of the best, if not the best heroin dealer in Boston. His clients were mostly of his friends and white suburban working class adults. However, the best of his quality was making sure I got my money for the heroin I gave him. Doug had a severe foot problem that caused him to walk as if walking on blistering hot coal. For a dope fiend, though, he had a modest heart.

Doug lived with his gay partner, Lamont, who was also an addict and whose skin was dark brown and as smooth as cashmere. In addition, her Jheri-curled hair due which touched the tip of her shoulders, was forever styled. In the days past, before Lamont landed a bookkeeping job at the John Hancock Life Insurance, in Boston, she went around dressed in drag, giving men the sensation that he was a she.

During the day, Doug spent most time at home dealing. Therefore, in the late afternoon, when Lamont got home from work, she'd take over, while Doug took off for either Suffolk Downs racetrack or Wonderland dog track. We'd often teased him of having two habits—heroin and gambling.

My children and I still had a good relationship. Thus, on Sunday afternoon I took my oldest daughter, who was going to be graduating from Memorial High that May and on her way to college to study "secretary of science," thought the flea market at the Cyclorama Building in the South End, an ideal place to shop for her graduation gift from me to her. Terry felt by shopping at the Cyclorama flea market that she'd find something no one else in her graduation class would have. Like me, she found flea markets ideal places to shop, especially if looking for something conservative. My interest then was mostly in the African American art during the time of Reconstruction, the Jim Crow, and sharecropping era. Nevertheless, I also had a thing for antique furniture, fine wood and jewels.

My daughter first wanted to look at the classical dresses on display hoping to find one in her taste and suited to wear at her prom. She truly hoped to find a dress she liked; and when she didn't, we both felt quite disappointed. Slowly we moved about the variety of booths, passing and stopping and taking to heart all the urbanity items on display. At one of the jewelry booths, where antique brooches, rings, necklaces … were displayed. The adornments were mostly set in Victorian setting. There she looked at a variety of pieces like a kid in a candy store. However, her interest in the many pieces, we moved on empty handed.

We were just about to complete the entire horseshoe—the shape the vendors' had their booths displayed; when I noticed that Terry was a bit melancholy at that point because she hadn't found her gift. Just then, she came to a dead stop in front of another jewelry booth, only a few feet away from the front exit.

"Daddy!" she bellowed, pointing to a gold watch in the showcase, "look at this one!" My first glance was at the women behind the booth whom I also found to be a jewel, and then at the watch my daughter was admiring and still pointing at with her finger.

"Look at this one Daddy!" pointing to a woman's gold rectangle antique watch with a black velvet band.

"You like that one, honey?" I asked, as I inhaled a nose full of an onion aroma coming from the food stand near by.

The woman looked like a flower child, and wore an assortment of silver rings on her every finger didn't hesitate in sliding open the showcase and gingerly removed the watch. She passed it to Terry with her left hand while brushing her long, thick red, hair from her face with the other. I stole another glance at her; and that time she busted me and smiled. However, it wasn't I whom she was interested in, it was in making and closing the sale.

"How's business so far?" I inquired.

"Okay, but it isn't at all as I'd like it to be."

"Well, the afternoon is still young," I said. I helped Terry buckled the black velvet strap around her wrist, and slowly she swayed her hand from side-to-side in admiration.

"That's what I want Daddy!" she insisted, as she continued swaying her hand from side-to-side and smiling down at her gift. It was a great decide, and I complimented her on her taste. I helped her out of the watch and gently passed it to the woman who placed it in its black velvet watch casing with a crimson velvet interior. I paid for the watch and Terry and I made it over to an Italian food stand, and each ordered Italian sausage and onion subs.

Before leaving, I left Terry in the food section and quickly made it back to an antique furniture booth where I'd earlier bought a replica Queen Ann angel-wings chair newly upholstered in a gold colored, flower patented fabric. Since my interior decorating courses, I always wanted an angle-wing chair. The young man, with feminine qualities and a great attitude, which I'd purchased the chair from carried it out to the car, placed it in the trunk; then, tired the trunk down with twine.

The next day I brought Doug another package of heroin and picked up my money from the previous one. Sitting in a chair near the bed, and next to the bay window with their shades raised midway, was this appealing brunette sporting a Peter Pan haircut, looking a bit boyish, and causally, but expensively dressed. As she boosted the speedball back and forth into a vein in her puffy right hand. She nattered lively about both her recent trip to Porto Rico and her night before, at the Pussy Cat strip joint, in the Combat Zone, where she'd worked as an exotic dancer. She didn't give Doug, or Lamont or the white couple, sitting on the bed getting off, a change to inter a word. Yap, yap, and yap she went on.

From what I could make of her, she was attractive and dressed both ravishingly and expansively. Yet, her puffy hands robbed her of some of her beauty. She had already used up her veins or else she certainly wouldn't have been getting off in her manicured hands.

As a boss, I spoke only to Doug and Lamont and said nothing to the other three persons present in the crammed studio apartment. The studio had a very narrow kitchen with stove, dishwasher, refrigerator, and a rolling metal stand, which contained a variety of spices. The bedroom/living room was just a tiny bit larger than the kingside bed, which occupied it. Before leaving, I learned from Doug that her name was, Mimi and that she was either thirty-two or three.

A few days later, again when I stopped by Doug's I Found Mimi there, sitting on the bed nattering none stop. It was Saturday morning and Lamont was home for the weekend, and Doug played with his big friendly shaggy and red colored chow dog, lying on the bed near him. Everybody was full of good spirits, and satisfaction.

Lamont who sat in the sofa chair near the bay window got up and gave it to me, and went sat on a kitchen chair across the room. Mimi picked up her purse and went into the bathroom. She made an about-face and returned for her cigarettes and lighter.

"Be careful shooting that shit!" Doug warned Mimi. "You know what happened to you a few weeks ago. It took Lamont and me all we know, to bring you out of that overdose!"

"I'm just going to use the bathroom," Mimi smiled at us.

It was a superb spring morning and Lamont had the three bay windows fully opened and the curtains thrown back, allowing light to fill the room with a country likeness. The trees and the ones near the windows were gradually getting dressed in their foliages and the air smelled green and fresh. Mimi stepped out of the bathroom, and we could tell that she had gotten off again. For, she had that euphoria sunshine smile on her cared face; which said, I'm high, lustrous, and bold. I liked that in a woman.

She promenaded over to where I sat squeezing her way through the small space between the bed and bureau and seated her firm bottom on my lap, quickly wiggled it from side-to-side; then, looked at me inquisitively to see what I thought of her, and her boldness. I said nothing; hell, she was hip, beautiful, well kept, had money, and lived in Brookline—and shot dope, too. Now, since moving up in my dealings and separated from Marcia I need a *woman* who had some class, knew the game, or street life and would look good at my side. She was it.

Mimi stood up, smiled down on me, "You must be from out of town?" I knew she was only being modest, for I'm quite sure that Doug and Lamont had told her as much about me as they told me about her.

"Oh, I've been around," I said looking into her eyes, where she now sat on the bed's edge across from me, with our legs lightly touching. She and I were both feeling the heroin through and through out our body. Moreover, we spoke softly and bubbly best we could because Doug still had to serve his morning customers that kept his phone ringing off the hook. Only Doug and Lamont's friends and costumers were welcome to come to their house to buy dope—the rest of his customers, which were few he served in the street, at certain locations in the area. Mimi told me that she'd just gotten fire from her stripped dancing job at the Pussycat Lounge for taking off too many days.

The Pussycat was a strip joint in the Red Light district, once known, by travels, nationwide and across the seas as the "Combat Zone" in Boston's China Town.

"Yeah," she said, "but I know the owners at the Mousetrap, a strip club at Park Square. You know the place?" I knew of the place.

Every time I looked around, she was lighting a fresh cigarette. She chain-smoked like most heroin addicts. The two seemed to go hand-in-hands. When Mimi stood up, I observed just how superb and firmed her body had sculptured from dancing.

"Would you like to take a ride to Brookline with me?" She flirtatiously said fun-lovingly, as she took her hand and gently massaged me beneath my chin. "I want to show you something," she said enthusiastic slipping into her brown, butter soft leather, waist length jacket.

"Wow!" I blurted as we climbed in to the brown Cadillac, which still smelled branded new. "You got the whole world in your hands."

Mimi quickly sucked in three or four puffs of smoke, into her lungs, from her cigarette, before she got into the car, deeply inhaled it; and then, flicked the butt onto the street.

"It's my sugar daddy's car," she said, starting the engine; then, pushing in the cigarette lighter. As soon as it popped out, she rushed it up to the tip of her cigarette and lit it. "Yeah, he also bought the house in Brookline and placed me on the deed as half ownership."

When she told me the name of her sugar daddy and the club he own in the Combat Zone, I was somewhat taken by surprise because I'd known Johnny. In the early 1960s, I oftentimes hung out in his bar, the 663, on Washington in the Zone, talking to him. We never spoke of anything specific just small talk. Most of the times I was high off cough syrup, or Robitussin A-C and marijuana, but that were in the days before my heroin addiction. Johnny spoke to everyone, no matter the color or status, in a very respectful manner. He was and excellently listener and communicator. However, as I looked at it, he did have the making of a trick, a rich sugar daddy, lonely, and lacking in looks.

Whenever I entered the 663, Johnny was forever sitting at the far-end of the, dimly lighted bar. Moreover, it seemed as though he wore that same clothes daily—a pair of black slacks that shinned from wear and a dark brown polo style sleeveless shirt, which highlighted the Italian olive-skinned and chubby face. As we drove past the many commercial stores on Harvard Street, in Brookline, Mimi continued nattering about her sugar daddy the way any other prostitute would had talked about theirs. That if they were favorable enough to have one. Mimi was care for by her benefactor as if she were a Geisha girl.

She went on boasting that he spoiled her with money and gifts, and how respected he was towards Shanwda, her daughter. He gave her expensive jewelry to a full-length mink coat, with her initial engraved within. Johnny, she said took her to exceptional restaurants and on costly trips. All she needed to do, on occasion, was be with him, once and a while, and let him come to her bed, every Friday night, once a week.

Mimi and her sugar daddy didn't live together. Johnny in his early fifties still lived in the suburb, with his bossy old, over protective sister, whom forever tried picking his women for him. She certainly despised Mimi and thought her no more than a whore, a "hussy."

If a hooker, was favorable enough to get a sugar daddy, or a rich trick that meant she was the envy of not, only the prostitutes and hookers, but the women on calls that hid under the pretense of the escort services. A courtesan, with a sugar daddy dated and slept only with her sugar daddy. While the rest of her cotemporaries slept with multiple men in the course of a day.

Nevertheless, if she wanted coitus, which she craved, she had to go else where for it. From what I learned from the women of the night, is that nine out of ten sugar daddies didn't satisfy their Jezebels in bed.

Mimi pulled the caddy into her driveway and parked in front of the dilapidating garage. We exit the car and passed between, a forty-foot dumpster already fill with rubbish from the interior renovation of her large gray Victorian home and garage, a budding pear-tree, which rise beyond her third floor's, back porch. We entered the house from the basement, and up the narrow Victorian back stairway, with paint peeling from the wall, we climbed stepping over sheetrock, pealed wallpaper, and chips of paint. On the second floor, Mimi pushed opened the unlocked door, and we both entered the kitchen.

The first thing that caught my eyes, were the designer-formed maple wood cabinets, which complimented at least ten feet of kitchen wall space. My eyes spanned the surrounding; then, moved casually back over the vista to the focus point, which in that case was a large two-door white refrigerator with the icemaker dispenser in the door.

Next to the dinning-room door, sitting in a corner near one of the kitchen's windows that illuminated the room with bright daylight, was a small butcher-block table with two canned-seat chairs. The stainless steel sink and dishwasher area were, separated from the table by a small island. Moreover, the vibrantly variegated *scindapsus* plants, which resembles the *Philodendron* plant hung from two bright windows above the sink.

"Nice? Huh?" Mimi said with a smile of approval on her face.

"Yeah, they've done a great job; I like it."

"Then let me show you the rest of my house."

From the kitchen, we stepped into the dinning room, where I found it aesthetically challenging. For here, the room's picturesque sky-blue painted walls with their frames painted white I didn't particular like that design, for I found it too European for Boston's condo boom: space, light, color, plants, and a rustic and modern mixture of furniture.

Nevertheless, I did care for the dining room pecan wood table, flanked by four pecan chairs, complimented by two armchairs, which took command at either ends. For backdrop, across from her eloquence table set, stood a most outstanding high polished, pecan wood beak front cabinet, stacked neatly with fine bone china.

"Now, that's nice," I said staring up at the chandelier, which hung over the table.

"Ah huh," Mimi said, nattering on about how expansive both the table and front cabinet were.

There was also an enchanting chandelier, smaller than the one in the dining room hanging in the front entrance hallway, subsequently to the wall-to-wall carpeted living room, with its large bow windows. A fireplace, and a fiberglass bar stacked with booze gave the living room a welcoming feeling.

The furniture in the living room were of a large, sofa with a large floral, tan patented print, on medium background were posh and contented. To praise the large sofa a piece of bold, thick rectangle cut glass, five feet in length, sat on two bulky marble blocks. While, near the fireplace sat a deep brown intimidating leather comfy chair, which I assumed to be that of her sugar daddy. In the front of the sizeable room, with light pouring in from curtain less windows, and near the bow windows, stood the fiberglass bar stock with a show of booze and two tall chrome chairs, with fiberglass seats. As we toured the two bedrooms and unfinished bathroom, I asked her who lived on the first floor.

"Why, do you want to rent?" She said looking at me enticingly. "No, just asking."

"I'm only joking," she chortled. "My best friend, Joyce and her husband live down stairs, and no one lives upstairs, now that it hasn't been remodel."

When I announced my leaving, I could tell by the sudden lifting of her brow and the way she looked at me with regret on her face and surprised that I hadn't acknowledged her sexual alluring invitation. For that was her ache from the very beginning. Before taking off, Mimi asked would I call her later on that night. I answered that I was traveling to Louisiana, for five days, early the following morning; however, I promised to call her upon my returned.

"Is Doug going to have your stuff while you're away?" she asked hopefully. I explained to her that I was seriously considering letting go of my operation and going into the antique business when I returned to Boston. "Yeah, but it's easier for you to support your habit if you're in business for yourself."

Mimi didn't give a damn about how I support my jone—my heroin addiction. Hell, she thought that if she could fasten on to me, like a stag horn fern rooted to a tree, that I'd support her habit. Then, she'd have both sugar daddy and her own heroin pharmacist. It never crossed my mind, then, that

Mimi would later give up her sugar daddy to become my "Mimzee." Mimzee was a *nom amour*—or love name I'd given to her the first time we kissed. Moreover, she corrected anyone else, other than me who called her Mimzee.

"What I'm planning on doing," I said as we walk the long hallway back, through the kitchen, to its back door, "is buy some methadone from Conway and when I return I'd go on the methadone program. I'm serious about getting off heroin," I said convincing myself.

"Easily said than done, and you know that!" Mimi said.

Before dropping me off in front of Doug's apartment building, where my car was parked, she stopped at the elementary school on Harvard Street in Brookline to pick up her daughter, Shawnda, who she said was seven. Mimi also told me that Shawnda's father was an African American jazz musician whom Shawnda, at seven, had yet to meet. Most times, hookers themselves didn't know who fathered their children. So most times, they'd choose their pimp, or lover. Most will never admit that their trick is the child father, even if they know it one hundred percent; for they much rather have a baster-child than a trick-baby!

Shawnda was a Twiggy size child. Nonetheless, she was such a beautiful child and full of life. She had hazel eyes and long sandy blonde hair. One thing for sure, she certainly resembled her mother, who is white. When I stepped out the caddy parked behind my BMW, I gingerly shut its door. Mimi rolled down the passenger's window, reached forward and reminded me to call her upon my return.

FIFTEEN

A TRIP to LAFAYETTE

That night, before leaving town, I met up with my first cousin/brother, James, at the Colonial Lounge, on Tremont Street, across the street from the historical Slade bar & restaurant. James friends called him, Harry, "Dirty Harry," because he kept a .357 magnum in the trunk of his Chrysler New Yorker. I parked my car at Frederick Douglas Squares and crossed the street to the Colonial.

In the bar, I found my cousin and his buddies sitting and standing around at the far end of the long, dark-varnished bar; drinking and babbling. James was leaned about six one, six-2 with a butterscotch complexion, and somewhat resembled Billy D. Williams. The women saw this resemblance in him and sort him out as much as he did them. However, he was married to a wonderful woman who loved him wholly; though, that did not prevent him from womanizing. Sometimes, men don't see the important of a marriage until the pot is empty.

After James, me, and his friends had smoked some pot, snorted some coke, and party the night away, we all had to get up in the morning, them for work—me to travel. As I opened the car's door, James called out to me as he climbed into his car.

"Hay cousin—"

I barely heard what Jim said, because of the screaming serine of a police cruiser speeding by with blue lights flicking frantically in the night. "What did you say?" I called back, when the noise had passed. "Don't forget to tell my people hello for me."

I pulled myself out of bed around 4:30 a.m., shot my last three bags of heroin and promised myself that, this was my last, last fix. I had enough methadone to last ten days, but would be in Louisiana only five day. I had to make sure that I had more than enough. Hell, I certainly didn't want to be in Lafayette dope sick again. That had happened to me before, years ago, when I was on the road traveling and hustling. After getting off, I took a lengthy shower, and thereafter packed and prepared for the trip. My flight was schedule to leave Logan International Airport at 8:00 a.m.

I wasn't at all tired from the night before. Heroin was like that, it removed me from weariness and the long arms of anxieties. Moreover, a good heroin high, to me, was absolute bliss—no doubt about it. Therefore, it was for that feeling of absolute that I continued using heroin, over-and-over again. I was an addict terrified of letting my life catch up to me. To do so, meant that I had to again, face all my qualms and compulsions, all my anxieties, all my shame, and all my guilt. Life for me came from the cooker.

When I arrived at New Orleans Regional Airport, I transferred to a crop duster for the final trip to Lafayette. After flying the comfort of Delta, the small jet with its tight compartment seemed somewhat frightening. I did't know why I felt so apprehensive, for I'd been in a much smaller plane than that one. As the crop duster lifted into the clear blue sky, I suddenly got over my apprehension, sat back and enjoyed a smooth flight to Lafayette.

In Lafayette, I live with my sister, Betty, and found out that some of my old buddies still hung out on the Block in the red-light district, where I later met up with them. In addition, for the first few days, all my buddies and I did were party. However, I did get a chance to visit family and friends in New Iberia, the birthplace of both James and I, and where I spent the first four and half years of my life. There I passed along James' greetings to his mother and father, Aunt Daisy and Uncle Joe.

Since I'd already seen most of the persons I'd planned to meet, I just hung around Betty's, eating up all her Creole cooking. To me, my sister cooked the best T-bone stake in all of the country. I also feasted on crawfish stew, and crawfish boiled in Jax beer. Jax beer was a famous beer back then. Betty was a great cook; fixing me red beans and rice, served with fried chicken and potato salad. I also filled my chop with stewed catfish cooked in tomato sauce, served over long-grain rice … No, no! I would not have left Lafayette before filling myself with bowls of "file gumbo," one of Louisiana finest dish.

When I returned to Boston, I gave Mimi a call; and a few days later, I picked her up at the Mousetrap lounge where she danced as a stripper. It was 2:00 a.m., and the only place serving food still opened, was a late night pizza joint, in Park Square. Thus, we picked up a pizza and drove over to my place, in Roxbury, at Brigham Circle and the Brigham and Women Hospital.

At my tiny studio, which I styled with a friendly décor, using bright colors, natural light, blue carpet, and houseplants; therefore giving the studio an illusion of more space. I placed the two chairs, an orange director's chair and a Quaker wooden chair with arms, around the kitchen table that I'd purchased at the flee market. Mimi and I got off, smoke some pot, snorted some coke, drink some Bordeaux; and then, made some explosive love!

Like a hundred times before, I'd lied to myself about not using dope again. Heroin was my life, my orgasm. It was better than sex. Nothing at all pained nor worried me when I lay in her arms. She was my lover and my worst experience. After about an hour sleep we got up around 7:00 a.m., got off, and then I drove her home where she picked up her daughter from her friend, Joyce, who lived on the first floor, and went up stair to prepare Shawnda for school and feed her breakfast.

Again, I began flying in-and-out of New York City buying heroin. I made my trips, in the morning, along with the businesspersons who worked on Wall Street, the World Trade Center, and other businesses in the city. Once on the shuttle flight from Boston to New York, I read the Wall Street Journal, not only to fit in with the others but to also, learn the terminology of business and the going on in the world.

I never had a problem getting along with people of any culture. I believe that people, all people no matter their status or ethnicity or color, are just people. Moreover, I dressed well, was well read in both periodicals and literature, and all sorts of textbooks. Moreover, I was intelligent and pleasant, handsome, with smooth reddish-brown skin, medium built with a yoga toned body, and move with conviction. I had no problems with communicating.

Once at LaGuardia, white cabdrivers who drove me to Harlem would never take me where I needed to go, which was 127th Street and Lenox Avenue, then, a hellhole with high crime, dilapidated-buildings and a dismal atmosphere. It was a lair for crime, junkies, dope dealers, and bums. White cabdrivers, for fear of robbed or worst, would not dare go past 125th Street and Lenox Avenue or anywhere else in Harlem.

Refusing to take me farther, I'd walked the two New York blocks up Lenox and turned right onto 127th Street. In the middle of the block on the right hand side of the street, I entered one of the brownstone buildings where the walls on either side of the stairways, where perhaps, a long time ago had been painted an antique white. However, from cigarette smoke grime, and who knows what else, the walls look similar to Harlem's back allies.

The once black and white ceramic, checkered, tiled floor and garnet stairs leading to the above apartments had been mopped so often with muddy water that the only part of the floor and stairs that weren't covered with muck, were the very center of the floor and stairs, where persons walked-up-and-down, and-back-and-forth. It felt as if I were spiraling up a narrow downed, mountain path to my connections. Yet I could tell by the design and the architect that many moons ago, it was once a majestic building for the rich Whites, and many years later for the rich Black minds and that of the poor Black residents of the "Harlem Renaissance." By the early 1960s Harlem begun producing heroin addicts and squalors and drug dealers so suddenly that it caught New Yorkers unprepared to deal with the heroin problem. Back then, there were as many white addicts as black and Latinos addicts in the City.

As I followed, the path up to the third floor the stench of urine became more concentrated with each step, to the point where my eyes burned. When reaching the third floor apartment I gently knocked on the earth-brown painted, heavy metal door, where my connections dealt their dope.

A few second passed; then, I'd hear that pleasant voice of Ella, "who's there?"

"It's Elow," I'd whispered; knowing that she was expecting me. For I'd called her before leaving Boston, letting her know I'd be there within the hour or so.

Ella, unlock the smallest locks first, then the two deadlocks. Finally, she'd unlock the major lock—the steel-door police lock—which crossed the center, breadth, of the door and resembled the steering wheel, "Club" lock. She opened the door, and her beautiful plump body and corn-flak colored face greeted me with joy and a big friendly smile that seemed permanently fixed to her round face. I followed behind her as we mosey down the lengthy corridor, passing two bedrooms, the bathroom, and kitchen all clean and orderly arranged, to her elaborately living room—decorated in Iris hue. Everything was purple. The soft carpet beneath my feet, the sofa and the, quiet purple painted walls, and the thin pastel purple curtains, blowing inwardly from a March breeze coming in through open windows.

There she'd invited me to sit while she went into her bedroom, which was juxtaposed to the living room. In just a moment, she'd emerge with my dope and I'd gave her, her money. Then, follower her back down the hallway to her "Forth Knox" door—that's what Ella and her man, Richard call it. Things always went well with our deals whether I dealt with Ella or Richard. Nevertheless, Ella and I took care of business and I was out of there. It took me two-and-a-half hours to fly from Boston to the City and back.

SIXTEEN

MOVING in with MIMI

Not long after my moving in with Mimi, we gave up our dealers and began dealing for ourselves, right there, out of our Brookline home. With my moving in, I persuaded Mimi to give up both her dancing profession and her composed sugar daddy, for I had an idea that we could become a real family. Maybe that was exactly what I thought I needed a new and fresh family. I could have gone back to Marcia if I wanted to, for she called me every night my first three months with Mimi, in favor of my returning home.

Marcia was always optimistic—she always felt that if I changed my addiction lifestyle our lives together would be a far better one. However, for me to go home would not be the right thing for me to do. I was shooting dope 500 hundred miles an hours. At anytime, I could find myself, busted and locked down in the penitentiary, leaving her and the children again. Hell, she had a sugar daddy to take care of her. He would have given her the last penny in his pocket, for him it was blind love.

For years, she and the children lived off him whenever I was not around. Wolf, her sugar daddy, was hard working, loved Marcia deeply, and would take good care of her and the children. All he needed is for me to get out of the picture. However, Marcia really did not want him but had no better choice, for she needed help raising four children. Some twenty-years after our divorce Marcia and Wolf were married. They were married in 2002 nine-months after I was released prison with my life changed from a street junky to a God fearing man. Wolf saw the change in me and was afraid that Marcia and I would again get back together; thus, he hurried up, and married her. Even so, it was over between Marcia and me.

However, that was my junkie Ideology at work thinking of a new and fresh family start. Like most times, I was thinking from a heroin point of view. I really wanted to be responsible; but my soul buried itself in the black pit of hell. In her heroin point of view, Mimi as well visualized a family thing between the three of us. Because she did gave up her stripping and dismissed her sugar daddy. Thus, we began our common-law marriage. Our heroin dealing was bringing in lots of dollars because we no longer had to give Doug forty percent of the profit: pay for a top-notch dealer. Furthermore, Doug was one of my best friends and him, along with the rest of my friends who were mostly pimps, hustlers, dope dealers, and junkies, called me an idiot ... for having Mimi give up her sugar daddy. They accused me of throwing away "trick money," and weak on pimping.

I never wanted to be a pimp. playing and stealing were my practice. If I'd wanted to be a pimp, I could have been one at age seventeen, when Marcia, my former wife, told me one night that she'd do anything for me, even go out on the street. One of her best friends was already out there. I looked at Marcia, who was so young, warm and beautiful and childlike; and said, "No!" for I loved her that much and knew with all my heart that she loved me.

In addition, if I wanted to, I could have turned her into a junkie as well. Marcia was special to me and, I really wanted a good life with her. I wanted her to be my wife and to bear my children; and indeed, she did. Today, all four of our children are college graduates; and my only son, Darryl Elow, who I wish will give me a grandson someday, has a PhD. in Mystic Theology [Boston University]. I give the honor to Marcia for her motherly strength and nutrient. The children you, see, are my seeds; and I thought them, early on in their lives, the impotent of both education and higher education. I had to teach them quickly whenever I was around, for I did not know where I'd be tomorrow and tomorrow and tomorrow.

Johnny, Mimi's sugar daddy, who was worth more than a million dollars, would have given Mimi whatever she asked for. Nevertheless, I had what she lust for more than money, more than her daughter, and more than my love, I had the bag, or the heroin. Dealers out of New York began calling heroin "P-funk" when heroin went from ten dollars a bag, to forty dollars a bag. The country was in a heroin deficiency from the late '70s to the mid '80s, when heroin dropped back down to ten dollars a bag.

"Say man you got any that P-funk?" went the street lingo. Though we were strung-out, and drug dealers, too, Mimi and I lived our lives like any other middleclass family in Brookline. We even went to church on Sundays; hoping to find faith—which we hoped, would rein us in from our preposterous behavior—and to continue raising Shawna, whom had recently made her First Holy Communion, as a Catholic.

That May, for Mother's Day, Mimi wanted me to take her to New York City; thus, we made reservation to stay at the Grand Hyatt Hotel. When arriving in New York City, we parked the Audi in a nearby parking garage and took a cab to the hotel. Moreover, when we pulled up in front of the Grand Hyatt, limousines lined its front drive-through entrance while voyagers exit them like bourgeoisie show-dogs; then, sauntered on into the hotel.

A young bellhop, of Asian descent, with a yellowish complexion and soft girlish manner, opened the door for Mimi, while I got out on the other side. The cabby had flipped a switch on the dashboard, which caused the trunk to pop open. The bellhop gracefully removed our bags and loaded them onto a luggage-cart. When Mimi and I walked into the sumptuous hotel lobby the first thing I noticed was, the large tropical plants that were majestically placed here-and-there in golden planters. To the right of me was the bar; and while Mimi checked us in, I mosey on up to it and order a double shot of Vodka with orange juice. Next to the bar was an exquisite sun-porch where persons with the look of jovial written on their face sat at tables covered with white lining cloth. Hanging from dark brown and wooden ceiling beams, where the common vine: *philodendrons*, the marble queen, and grape and English ivies.

A couple hours after we settle into our hotel room, I removed from one of the traveling bags an envelope containing money. I got off on a half spook of heroin, kissed Mimi who was sitting on the bed with her back propped up against a cluster of pillows, reading her favorite *People Magazines*. Once outside, I walked a short distant up Lexington Avenue. I chose not to take a cab from the hotel because I assumed that cabbies parked in front were regulars there, and I didn't want either of them knowing that I was going to Harlem. For the very question in their mouths might be, "What's a nice clean fellow like you doing going to Harlem?"

No, I didn't want anyone wondering about my intentions, other than being in New York with my wife to have pleasant time. I really didn't need those cabbies that were regulars at the hotel, in my business. One thing about good cabbies in any City, they're often aware of what's going on around town.

On Lexington Avenue, I grabbed a New York Taxi and told the driver who resembled Humpty Dumpty, and wearing a Moa's cap on his head, my destination. He turned his broad body around, and gave me a hello smile. "I go far as a 125th Street and Lenox, and that's it," he said, apologetic.

"That sounds like a good stop, to me," I answered adjusting myself to the seat as he crept back into the Saturday afternoon traffic. The common people on the streets of Harlem, like always, were as busy as humming birds, as they gathered up neuter for their daily living. They were living in tough times, for New York black gangsters had Harlem caught in a wolf's trap, where murdered bodies laid on streets trough out the City!

Heroin and death suffocated the City, leaving the common people petrified of going out into the streets and more petrified for their children. In the '70s and '80s the black gangsters controlled most of the dope in Harlem, if not all; and they eradicate all that got in their way. In addition, here I moved right there among them in the mixer of invisible insanity, and believing that I wasn't ready to die.

The wind had picked up some velocity and pushed against my back, as I walked up Lenox toward 127th Street, wishing to get out of Dodge as soon as possible. All along Lenox Avenue, the vendors had their concession stands lineup on either side of the street; selling everything from clothing, to boil crabs. There was even a concession stand selling peanut butter and jelly sandwiches for seventy-five cent, each. "Hay my brother!" barked the, doped up, peanut butter man with long fingernails pointing at his small table where sat an old stove-pot with a black liquate inside it. Moreover, on his head was a soiled and stand summer, golf hat that could have once been light-colored, pulled down, to his ears, over his thick afro. "I got some hot coffee to go with that P&JS." I laughed and mocked, to myself, over what he had just said, and kept moving.

Then there were the panhandlers asking for spare change, while the boosters—shoplifters, moved through the crowd selling their stolen goods. The junkies, the ones who were already high, just stood on the sidewalk nodding to the point that if you didn't know better, you'd think they were doing Thai Chi.

A booster with a berry black complexion, a face moist and grease, with a mucky odor coming from him, and huge puffed up hands; which looked like they were ready to burst, approached me and asked, If I wanted to buy four cases of crab meat.

"Where's the crab meat? " I asked the brother, not that I was interested in buying. "You know that if you had four cases of crab meat, you wouldn't peddle them on the streets. Any store in the neighborhood would fence them from you." I rounded, or ignored the dude and turned right off Lenox onto 127th Street; went to my connection, purchased my lot of heroin from the plump and lustrous Ella and left. To purchase cocaine, I had to go up to 138th and Lenox to my Dominican coke dealers. Outside I held down a gypsy cab and exited it at a 138th and Lenox. I move down 138th Street toward my connection place passing junkies and drunks, who were so filthy that they looked as if they were chimneysweepers. Then there were these dilapidated buildings, on other either side of the street. Some boarded up while others looked as if General Paton had come through with his army.

The building I entered was as dilapidated as the other ones I'd just past. The front door hung inward supported only by its bottom hinge. In the hallways, the order of cat urine and the aroma of supper cooking, in the many apartments, fought for first place.

I cautiously ascended the stairs to the third floor and knocked on the door facing the stairs I'd just climbed. There was no answer, again I knocked; then, a third time, still no answer. Just as I was about to walk down the stairs, I heard the door-locks on the adjoining apartment door being un-locked. When it opened a middle age chubby, no, fat, Latina woman with olive skin, wearing an ankle-length bathrobe with, a big embroiled sunflower pinned to its top.

"They up there," she pointed a finger up to the floor above and yelled in Spanish to someone. A male voice yelled back down in Spanish. "They come in few minute, she said."

"Thank you," I said, as she backed into her apartment and began clicking locks shut.

A few minutes passed and three grinning brown-face Dominicans descended the upper floor. Two of the [cowboys] carried, .357 Magnums in their hand. The short stocky one who had the biggest grin on his face carried a small measuring scale in his right hand and a plastic bag fill with coke in the other. One of the cowboys unlocked the three locks and we all entered the apartment. The living room had no furniture and the heavy dark curtains in the windows blocked most of the day light from entering. Passing through the living room, we entered a small room, where someone turned on the light. The room had one window entirely covered with a soiled yellow sheet.

The only furniture in the miniature coalminer, looking room was an old rustic wooden chair and a tiny wooden table. The cowboy, who'd unlocked the front door, stood with his back against the closed door blocking its exit, while the other stood behind the table with his back facing the window, looking like a grinning eunuch. The one handling the drug, the boss, sat at the table and began weighing my order. Not once did the three lose their grin.

"Man, look," I said. "When are you going to trust me enough to stop pulling guns out when I'm here?" The two holding the guns didn't understand a word of English, but the boss spoke it fairly well.

"Don't worry, amigo, you safe," said the boss. "Next month we bring you the coke in Boston."

"You're coming to Boston?"

"Next month we coming to Boston for visit; we bring it to you."

"Come and I'll show you a great time!"

"A Deal," he said with his eyes on the scale. Back on the streets of Harlem, I waved down a gypsy cab and had her drop me off at 110th and Fifth Avenue. There I switched to a NYC Taxi for the trip back to the hotel; and once there I went over to the bar and downed a shooting and chilled Screwdriver, double shot, before taking the plushy elevator to the room.

SEVENTEEN

IN NEW YORK CITY WITH MIMI

In the room, I found Mimi upset about forgetting to pack her hairbrush. I calmed her down while we both snorted a few lines of coke and got off. After getting high, I went down to the lobby's gift shop and as luck would have it, I walk directly to the hairbrush showcase and bought the first lady bush I saw. I paid the clerk, a young lady in a marvel frame of mind, and eased over to the bar where I hooked up with a double shot of Vodka and orange juice for a brief moment; then, went up to the room. As long as I was snorting coke, I could drink an unbelievable amount of booze, party all night long, and not get drunk.

Back in the romantic room of aura, I gave Mimi the hairbrush, which the clerk had put in one of those cute little colorful bag; moreover, when she removed that brush, from the bag, her brown eyes widen and shorn as if they were glazed enamel. She removed the price tag from the tortoise-shell brush and gave me a long deep kiss, whereas our tongues played a lustful melody.

"Let's hold on to this passion until after we party," Mimi said gently pushing me away as she dropped her robe to the floor and entered the bathroom. Dropping her robe to the floor was one of her ways of teasing me.

As we both dressed for the night out—party—as Mimi called it, we on occasions would zipped up to the bureau where we snorted a line or two of coke; then, proceeded to dressing. After I'd gotten dressed, I filled two mini coke-vile with coke. That's the way Mimi wanted it. She wanted her own vile that way she'd have hers own coke.

Outside, in front of the hotel, the door attendant signaled to the first cab waiting in line in front of the hotel. "This cabby knows all the best places in the City," said the door attendant, stealing a glance at my flamboyant Mimzee. Who was dressed in a low-cut black evening dress, wearing diamond-linked earrings on her ears and around her lick-able neck hung a single diamond, which complimenting her creamy white bust. "You guys have a good time," the door attendant continued, as I passed him his tipped and entered the cab.

"Boy, he's tall," Mimi, said of the door attendant.

"You should have seen how large his hands were," I said jokingly.

"Yeah," Mimi declared. "I bet you filled them with a large tip, too." I always tipped well; at least twenty-five present in restaurants, which annoyed Mimi.

The cab driver, who was in his mid sixty, with a white head of hair shortly chopped, and a watermelon belly, which rubbed against the steering wheel as he steered in and out of New York's nightlife traffic, said in a neighborly voice, "I know just the spots." He answered when Mimi told him our preference for the night. "I know just the Jazz and Disco spots for you, and you'll see you'll enjoy y'all-selves."

It was just passed midnight when the, cabby dropped us off at a jazz club on the Upper East Side; and then suggested that he would pick us up in a couple hours and drive us over to the Disco lounge, which he'd chosen for us to have a dancing goodtime.

The jazz club had little lighting in it. In fact, most of the lighting in the club filtered in from the streetlights on 5th Avenue. The club was a tiny spot and the atmosphere truly jazz, where a tall sleek, root-beer complexion woman in her early thirties, wearing a sleeveless black gown that showed every curve of her sleek seductive body, sung old school jazz. While an old timer with a thick silvery manicured mustache, softly fingered the piano keys, and the drummer lightly scratched at the drum, with drum fans.

Before we realized it, it was already 2:00 a.m., and the cabby had entered the club letting us know that he'd be outside waiting. The Disco joint was jammed packed and jelly-tight. Moreover, we had to squeeze our bodies through a crowd of highly spirited people. The dance floor was pack wall-to-wall with dancers and over their heads hung a huge Roaring Twenties' ball, which spun around-and-around, casting its silvery ray upon the dancers.

We found a tight space in the back of the lounge and sat down on a bench that ran alongside of the wall. In front of the bench were miniature tables, about a foot apart of each other. Everywhere I looked, there were people, sitting or standing, laughing and drinking, dancing and just having a Disco good time. The club was just one gigantic room with a large circler bar in its center.

After a couple drinks and a noise full of coke, Mimi and I took to the dance floor. She was an excellent dancer. Me, I couldn't dance at all. However, once I filled myself with booze and drugs, I became one of the best dancers on the dance floor. On the dance floor that night, my body and feet went through motions I never thought I had in me. I moved gracefully to the music, as if on air. In addition, Mimi, with her fine self, shifted her sculptured and subjective figure according to my body rhythm. We were having a party of a good time.

When we stepped out of the lounge, the sky had turned gray with the light of dawn. We didn't bother to flag a cab, we just strolled down the street acting like teenagers, holding hands and bumping hips. When we did flag, a cab near Columbus Circle the sun was rising softly over the buildings in the East while the, morning, city's street sanitation trucks, wash down Columbus Avenue. Indeed, it was a wonderful Sunday morning, just wonderful. In the cab, Mimi tightly glued her body to mines; throw her legs over my lap exposing her firm thighs. She kissed me and thanked me for a great mother's day.

At the hotel we got off, bathed each other in the shower and went to bed, and there we fell asleep, but not before the outburst of our sexual delights. We slept a little over three hours; and after our morning fix and a few lines of coke, we climbed back into bed and again discharged in sexual fulfillment. We took a shower, dressed, and packed. For it was our intention to leave the City for Boston late Sunday afternoon. However, upon closing our account, on Sunday evening, we had to pay for Monday's bill as well because our check out period was for Monday at noon. We had to get back to business. However, before leaving New York, we were going to do some sightseeing, get something to eat, and do some shopping.

Upon exiting the hotel, we found the afternoon filled with blue-sky, not a cloud present. May's weather was treating us well; and because the day was so enjoyable, we decided to walk along Forty Second Street to Time Square, and then take a cab to Columbus Circle for a bite to eat.

As we walked past the many commercial shops, it was impossible not to have noticed a few shops' display widows partially eclipsed by homeless people, drug dealers and hookers, drunks and freaks. The hookers and the dealers occasionally stepped in-and-out of the shops' doorways where hookers gave quick blowjobs and where dealers dealt their drugs, and the drunks drink their wine. Time Square in the '60s up to the '80, was Sodom and Gomorrah—for real. Even so, that didn't stop most tourist from sighting seeing and loving every bit of if. They'd have something to tell their friends and family back home.

Out of nowhere, a hooker bumped in to the front of me and my first thought—*she's a pickpocket;* however she wasn't. Nevertheless, wow, boy, did she need a bathe—like right now. Now here comes an audacious streetwalker gaiting down the street jammed off heroin, who had the audacity to step in front of a priest, who was going about his afternoon affairs. She grabbed his crotch, with the quickness and said, "Come here baby and let me hear your confession."

I roared with laughter. Couldn't help it. Though Mimi tried keeping her tourist likeness in place, she too burst into laughter. The now red-face silvery hair, bifocal wearing priest who was dressed in collar gasped with surprise and wrenched him self free while nearly knocking down a group of pedestrians as he hurried toward Lexington Avenue.

The drug dealers, who thought themselves cool and untouchable, constantly took junkies in-and-out of shops' doorways serving them his poison. They'd look around nonchalantly making sure the law wasn't around and as quick as lightening make their sales. There were even persons in limousines, who'd pulled up to the curb. The dealer would climb into one door and exit out the other door. All kinds of persons bought dope on 42nd Street; doctors, lawyers, stockbrokers, housemothers, school youngsters, actors—and vagabonds too.

Hell, just last night, at the Disco, Mimi and I were snorting coke with an undercover New York police detective. In addition, because he was a cop he got his coke snorts from the partygoers for nothing. I rather liked him, though. However, I also knew that as soon as he went back on duty, he wouldn't hesitate to arrest a coke head caught snorting coke in an ally, or a sick junkie trying to get his first morning fix. That's one of the reasons why some people called cops, "pigs," in those days.

As fast as the dealers served three or four junkies, there was as many waiting. Moreover, who knows, there could also have been an undercover waiting in line to make an arrest. He could even be our Disco coke-snorting detective. 42nd Street was just one large freak show, where both the idiots and the furies spent their mortal time.

When we reached the center of the world—Time Square—it brought back old memories of when I lived and hustled in Manhattan during the '60s. In fact, I lived right down the street at the Hotel Dixie, in Time Square. There I used to enter the hotel lobby through the front door, on 42nd Street, but frequently exit it through the side door that led to 43rd Street, just across the street from *New York Times*. Every time I exited the hotel's side door and looked at the *Times'* building, I said to myself, *Wow, the New York Times!* It fascinated me to know that I was staying next door to one of the largest and greatest newspaper publishers, in the world.

In the '60s the pimps and hustles from Boston hung-out in bars and poolrooms from Time Square, to West 77th Street. Our favorite poolroom was the Gays and Dolls on 7th and 50th Street. Moreover, our favorite bar and diner was the Copper Rail on 7th Avenue across the street from the Brass Rail—go, go, Lounge.

After-hours, when the women of the night had gathered in their harvest of money for their pimps, the pimps and hustles, along with their women hung out for breakfast at the "Ham and Eggs" which was near Needle Park, on the corner of Amsterdam Avenue and 74th Street.

After lunch at, Fridays, we took a cab to 5th Avenue for a carriage ride through Central Park. The young woman in charge of the horse carriage was a plump blonde-haired person with a charming round face and a smile, which said, "Hello." When we seated ourselves, I asked the carrier to raise the carriage's top. She tugged at the black-canvas top until she finally got it up and over us.

As the whitish, grayish horse that had applied itself, over the years, to pulling carriages, soon dropped its head down low and slightly to the left, as it clicked clacked along the pavement through Central Park. I pulled from the pocket of my blue Chinese silk jacket, a vile of coke. When opening the vial, I eased my coke spoon into it and snorted a couple hits of the white powder into each nostril; then, passed the spoon and vial to Mimi. At first, we were a bit skeptical about what the driver thought of our sniffling sound. Did she know? Yes, she knew. Not only was this New York City, but this was the era of both Disco and the psychedelic age, when almost everyone in America was getting high on one thing or another.

After taking pleasure in the ride, we walked along Central Park East, down 5th Avenue taking in the scenery while on our way back to the Grand Hyatt. On the Avenue, wrinkly gray men sat on benches near the Central Park wall. Some of the old fellows read newspapers, some daydreamed, while others fed pigeons that cluster the sidewalk and wildly scuttle to the sky in fright of rushing pedestrians.

After walking a few New York blocks, we took a cab to the hotel. Once there, while Mimi went to the desk to closeout our account; then, up to the room to gather up our luggage, I had the cabby take me over to the parking lot to pick up the Audi. By the time, I returned to the Grand Hyatt there was no sun seen in the sky, the cloud had turned a dark bluish gray, and impregnated with water. I parked the car in front of the hotel, and asked the door attendant to keep an eye out; then, dashed into the lobby and elevated myself to our room. As I entered the room, the attendant was exiting with our luggage placed on a pushcart.

From the hoarseness in Mimi's voice and the gracefulness of her body languish I could tell she'd just gotten off. When junkies got off on heroin, their personality changed and their voices picked up a pinch of hoarseness and their bodies radiated with a type of joy, which they thought they could find only in heroin. It was a world of elation; and they felt that they were at the top of their game, and equal to anyone else. However, huh, this is only a temporary triumph, for the conflicts and struggles that goes with being an addict—are always waiting just around the corner, to gobble him up.

"Where's mine?" I declared, hurrying to the bureau where Mimi stood. She opened one of the dresser's top drawers and pulled out a syringe containing my fix. Instead of wasting time looking for a vein, I dropped my pants, pulled down my boxers and skinned-popped, shot the dope into the muscle of my buttock.

Heroin is a vicious poison that robs the addicts of their sense of worth; it snatches their attention away from their present-day, family and friends; wife and children, church and God. Addicts become stuck in a server tornado that will kill them or spit them out, beaten to the bones. Yet many do find a way out.

When Mimi and I stepped outside the hotel, the door attendant had already popped the car's trunk and therein had placed our bags. He opened and closed the cab's door for Mimi, and turned to me with job well done, written across his smiling face. I tipped him, got into the car and gently wiggled my way onto Lexington Avenue, headed for the New York Turnpike. It was well past 8:00 p.m., and it looked like rain for sure. Consequently, just like that, before we could make it out of the city limit, the entire sky broke open and a, torrential rain came rushing down in enormous drops, as if to disinfect and wash the city of its sins. The rain was so brutal that we were unable to see the highway before us. Therefore, we took the first exit and found a nearby shopping mall and park in its parking lot.

Because of the pouring rain, we could hardly see the other cars parked juxtaposed us. Thus, we took advantage of our nature's-shaded windows, turned on the car's radio, got off, and then snorted some coke.

The junkie's life is no more than a pretension, a wanted-be, who cannot find his way to be or "not to be." He feels no comfort within himself; but some knows there's a talent buried deep within his being. He knows he's a lot more intelligent than his level of understandings. In addition, his lack of self-esteem keeps him down spirited.

EIGHTEEN

I SHOULD HAVE BEEN DEEPLY TOUCH

Mimi and I weren't anticipating the valley we were to find ourselves in. My wife, on the other hand called every night, asking me to come home, that she and the children missed me. Then there's Johnny, Mimi's had-been sugar daddy, coming at us with his demands. He wanted Mimi to sell her half of their home to him.

I explained to her that if she did decided to sell her half it would give Johnny the full right to evict us. The man wanted us out. Johnny had owned the 663 Lounge, gay bar, in the Combat Zone for what seemed like eternity, and had so much money that it poured out of every crack in the bar's walls. Thus, we believed him to be mob connected. Yet, even if he wasn't, Mimi knew that a great deal of people owed him favors; and he could have gotten just about any one of them to hurt or do us in.

I'd been in the streets most of my life, and had lived in it as, a daredevil. I was a challenger, ready for, even the mob; and death frightened me not. For I strongly believe what I'd once read in one of Carlos Castaneda's novels that, "death must struggle to take a worrier." So my street mind and dope fiend attitude really welcomed a confrontation with any one Johnny might send to retaliate—to give me a mob licking. Thus, I began carrying my small, .22 caliber semi-automatic pistols that I could easily conceal on my body. However, a fight between Johnny's people and me never materialized. Today

I wipe the sweat from my brow that Johnny hadn't set the mob on me, for I was no match for the Boston mob.

Now, on the other hand Marcia was bugging me. Every night around 8:00 she'd call, asking me to come home; "The kids and I need you," she'd say in a calm voice trying to convince me. The fact, I wasn't going back home. Mimi had asked me to marry her. However, before she'd asked, I'd already been talking to my lawyer about devoicing Marcia. A year or so later, she was served divorce papers, and did not argue the claim. I also felt she'd be a lot better off without me, for I hadn't changed my ways one iota. In fact, my ways had gotten worst. My addiction had gotten immeasurable, and we were selling heroin to addicts across the city of Boston, from the South End, Revere to Brighton/Allston and in-between, with ninety-five percent of our clients being of the working class; we hardly sold dope to junkies from the street.

I was touched that both my wife and children still wanted me home. Here I had a place to go, to where a loving family awaits me with unconditional love and hearts filled with forgiveness. I knew that I had a beautiful family, but heroin was irresistible, I loved her more than life. I would have died for heroin.

During the weekdays, Mimi and I stayed home slinging, selling heroin throughout the day and at It was so busy between 7:00 and 9:00 p.m. that we had to take the phones off their hooks, for twenty minutes, in order to have supper together. Nevertheless, without fail, the three of us gathered at the pecan table under the sparkling chandelier for supper each night.

On Friday nights, leaving Shanwda with the baby sitter, Mimi and I went out to play. We may have eaten at Veronique in Brookline or Du Berry on Newbery Street, maybe at the Empress Room at the Hyatt Hotel in Cambridge. After a pleasurable meal with wine, we usually ended up at a modest little nightclub on Commonwealth Avenue, on the Brookline and Brighton line to listen to soft Jazz, snort coke, drink wine, and eat pâté, with French bread.

A couple of times a month my two youngest daughters, Pam and Gwenette would stop by for their allowances. Terry and Darryl never came by; nevertheless, they too received their allowances that I sent them through Pam. Yet, I cannot remember a time when my children asked for money that I didn't have it to give. Once when Darryl, asked and I harshly told him he was now eighteen and time to begin earning his own money. I could see the anger mounting on his slender sensitive face as tears welled-up in his glassy brown eyes. Darryl never again asked me for money. That's how I wanted it to be. I wanted my son to learn early how to take care of himself. I wanted him to learn from that moment onward how to be a man capable of taking care of Darryl.

I was an addict and never knew when I might meet up with death from an over dose, or someone shooting me for breaking in his home. I just never knew when I'd be out of their lives. So whenever I was around them, I lived on the edge; for I had lots of work to do, I had to make sure that I took care of my habit first; then, the wellbeing of my family. To get the money to do that, I had to steal. I wanted my children to achieve both manners and higher education. I didn't want to see them stuck in the project for the rest of their lives. Thus, when I wasn't in prison or on the run from the police, I aggressively made it my business to teach them that life would be a lot better off with an education. If nothing else worked out between my children, and me the education part did. More important than education, I want them as well to love and respect their mother. They do to the present day.

By the time I met Mimi, and deserted my family, I'd already built in each of my children their frame of knowledge. All they had to do was fell them. Thank God, though, for there caring and nurturing young mother that each reached a place in their lives where they're doing well. While I lived in the black hold of the underworld, Marcia went right on raising the children in growth, order, and development. Something we both wanted for our children.

By the end of 1982, Mimi and I were still doing fairly well in the heroin business, but our money was slowly dwindling. The heroin in Harlem had gotten so bad, and weak that we sold less and less drug, and used more to keep our sickness at bay. I was flying in-and-out of New York every other day hoping to find a good package, but it seemed as though all the dope in the City was below par. The dope coming into Harlem at that time wasn't' enough to supply the street dealers and the junkies on the East coast. Thus, the dealers did what they always did when the dope in the City was weak they over cut it.

Not only were we having a hard time dealing weak dope to our customers and losing money; however, now that Johnny owned the house outright, he wanted us out but we went right on slinging our bad dope. After a while, the customers stopped coming by, and the phone stopped ringing and the flow of white gold, heroin, stop pumping. By then I was now flying in-and-out of New York once a week and the little dope I brought back, for the lack of money, was sometimes, just enough to support Mimi's and my habit.

By then I'd already begun breaking into people's, homes, and Mimi went back to stripping at the Mousetrap. The money made between the two of us went with the quickness, which caused us to begin liquidating our assets hoping to stay afloat. The first thing to go was the Audi, which we reported stolen and later collected the insurance money. Moreover, when the insurance money was all shot up, Mimi sold her, I. J. Fox full-length mink coat.

We certainly lived up to that old clichés: we sold everything in the house including the kitchen sink. Well we didn't sell the sink, but you know what I mean. The next thing to go was our jewelry, which were worth thousands of dollars. With that money spent, we moved on to selling the furniture, like the eloquent pecan dining room set. The Plexiglas-bar with its stools and all its bottles of booze went, too. We even sold the two doors refrigerator.

We were quickly sinking. Mimi had lost her job, and had now turned back to prostitution. Through our folly, Shawnda never went without, and went to school every day with her clothes pressed. Moreover, we still managed to send her to summer camp in the State of Maine every summer. However, Shawnda was no fool she was bright enough, at eight, to know that we were doing something wrong, and everyday her puzzle became clearer. A couple years ago, when Shawnda asked, Mimi, "Mama, what's that white power?" She would tell her daughter that it was part of her makeup. Mimi was then dancing; thus, she wore many types of makeup. However, Shawnda was growing and her thoughts were growing with her.

Our time was running out, for Johnny had taken us to court and the judge had given us ninety days to move out. Therefore, I went to see my friend, A. C. Hillman who rented a two-bedroom apartment in lower Roxbury, off Tremont Street. After alerting my friend of my plight, he invited us to take over the extra bedroom. However, he was concerned about the wellbeing of Shawnda who'd be exposed to, too many junkies going in-and-out of his house all day long. A. C. also managed a shooting gallery—where junkies pay to use the homeowner's home to get off.

Yes, Mimi and I were at our worse. As a prison saying goes, "One day chicken, the next day feathers." Hell isn't that just like life: The pro and the con, the protagonist and the antagonist, the tug-of-war, the temporary triumphs and the obstacles. The day we were to move, I left our Brookline home early that morning and went over to A. C's to make sure all was, still on, with use moving in. However, though I figured him my closest friend, he was a junkie first. In addition, junkies cannot be dependable. The words of a junkie are like butter under a hot August sun. I just had to make sure that before we moved our things we had a place to stay.

When I left the house, Mimi was still packing putting things into boxes and waiting for the Metropolitan Moving Company and storage to show up. On my way to A. C.'s I walked Shawnda, up Harvard Avenue to her school; then, jumped on the "T" for my mission to lower Roxbury. I arrived at A. C.'s around 7:00 a.m., and already two sick junkies, looking like zombies, standing over the kitchen sink. In the tiny weenie kitchen, preparing their morning fix while my man, A. C. stood over their shoulders, with that favorite Cheshire-cat grin written across his brownish yellowish skinned face, making sure that each junkie gave him at least 10cc's each of their heroin for the use of his apartment and works.

When addicts are cooking their dope as a group, they'd watch the person cooking it like a bird dog on the hunt, making sure they're not slipped a water-shot. They'd also make sure when that person drew up the heroin from the cooker, into the syringes, that each one got an equal amount. Junkies will beat their mother, who sometimes is the last person to give up on them; but then, she does it with a cleaver chopped heart. Junkies will rob their priest, stick up a judge, steal the "Jimmy Funs," committee violence crimes, and take from the dead. Like that early morning when, Andy Dean, a stick up thief and drug dealer, who had been found not guilty of two murder charges; got his dope by either selling it or robbing other dealers for their dope, was shot to death one early morning on Woodrow Avenue in front an oily booth-leg car repair shop and a dope fiend hang out.

A young dealer whom Andy had robbed just a week ago thought Andy had come back to the dope scene to rob him, again. The young dealer, who was about twenty years old, either in bravery or panic shot Andy as he stuck his hand into his pants pocket. The dealer shot him thinking he was going for his gun. As Andy fell onto the black oily concrete sidewalk, his hand exited his pocket, and slowly rested on the ground. In it was no gun, but instead a few dollars bills.

As Andy long thin corps laid in a pull of blood, in the warm morning sun, another junkie reached down, peeled Andy's fingers backward and removed the bills. There were twenty-nine dollars, enough to buy three bags of heroin with a dollar short. That morning Andy had his own money. That scene could have been any addict lying there, dead and partially covered with blood and oil.

After the addicts had gotten off in the tiny weenie kitchen, they were ready to run their mouths, but A. C. put both of them out, and then got off himself, leaving me a morsel amount. When we'd gotten off, he lit a joint, took a few pokes and passed it to me.

"Elow, man, you see how them perverts junkies come in and out of here at anytime," A. C. said dipping his knee and rubbing his nose. "Ohms," he went on, "man that was some good stuff, E, man, you can't live here. This isn't a place for Shawna to live." *What the hell am I going to do now?* I thought as a flood of anxiety rushed to my head. "But, I spoke to my sister, Diane," he went on after coming out of a nod, "and she's willing to rent you one of her bedroom along with the use of the house for ninety five dollars a week. She's crazy about how well she has decorated her front room; so that's the only place in the house that off limit to you."

I'd known Diane as long as I've known A. C., and really didn't want to live with her, for she'd a sexual thing for me, but I'd no desire for her and never took it farther than friendships. Thus, I knew right off that this wasn't a good idea to bring another woman into her house, to stay, especially a white woman. Nonetheless, I felt that I could handle Diane.

After we'd smoked up the joint, A. C. picked up from his neatly arranged dresser a sliver-colored ring with three keys dangling from it. He told me that one of the keys were for the front door and the other two were to Diane's apartment—and that it was all right to move in whenever I wanted to. He suggested we move in while his sister was at work. Diane lived in a row of newly developed buildings on Lenox Street directly across the street from the Lenox Street Housing Project—dopeville—and a block away from A. C. Even more, just two short blocks away from where my wife and children lived.

Diane's apartment was right in the center of the drug scene, Shawmut Avenue, a retreat for junkies, dealers, crack heads, and misfits were only a few steps away. In addition, Big Jim, Shanty Lounge, another place for junkies and misfits, was right around the corner, on Northampton and Washington Street. Junkies came from all over greater Boston and a lot farther to buy dope in that triangle. We would now be living in, dopeville, where dealers and their customers, and even some of the neighborhood residents, cared nothing about the decent people and their children who lived in the neighborhood.

NINETEEN

LENOX STREET APARTMENT

Before returning to Brookline, I thought it best, to go over Diane's apartment to check out the place. At the Apartment, front entrance, I unlocked the glass-door and entered the foyer. There I noticed the natural concrete interior walls and the stairway up. The stairway was quite spacious and made of gridiron, which caused the circulation of air to move freely about while the sharp geometric architectural design gave it a welcoming feeling.

I walked up the stairs to the second floor where Diane's apartment was located, unlocked the door and stepped in. "Damn." I heard myself saying as I shut the door behind me. The hardwood, high-polished stairway leading to the rooms above faced my direction, while the living room, with its blue-floral carpet, which complimented the neatly arranged furniture was to my right; and the small clean kitchen to the my left. The house was compact, but supper clean.

I climbed the stairs to the second floor and found it spotless as well. "Good," I exclaimed, as I peeked into the bedroom to my right. No, that was not my room. I then peeked into the bedroom to my left and that one was unmade. Our bedroom was small but when you're about to be kicked out into the street like a salon drunk, this was cool. Our Brookline home was sizable and lots of space for Shawnda to run around in. She often enjoyed provoking me to chase her through the large Victorian rooms. I guess most, if not all dysfunctional families have moments of temporary triumphs.

I left the apartment locking the door; then, walked down the stairs and out the front entrance, making sure the door locked shut behind me. As I'd come, I took the "T" back to Brookline, and when I arrived a crew of two men from Metropolitan were loading the last of the furniture onto the moving van to be stored in their warehouse in Cambridge.

In the house, I found Mimi locked away, from the crew, in our bedroom, sitting on the floor, trying to get off in a room, now, without furniture. "Is it okay for us to move?" she asked, as I moved across the room over to the bow windows, picked up the syringe from one of it's windowsill, which Mimi had prepared for me and proceeded to get off.

"We won't be living with A. C.," I said.

"What you mean?" Mimi exclaimed, about to have an anxiety attack. "You're saying that A. C. already changed his f... mind? I can't even find a f... vein to get off, and now we don't have a f... place to stay!"

"Give me a f... chance to finish what I'm saying!" I bellowed as I removed both shoe and sock from my right foot. Lately I had been getting off in a vein near my big toe. The vein fare in size and on my first try, I saw a speck of blood pop up into the bottom of the works, shoot straight to its top, and dissolved into the heroin, causing it turn a pinkish red. In school of interior design, I learnt that "pink" was "red," with the "fire" taken out. I thought that was clever.

I wasted no time and plunged the heroin forward feeling at once that rush, that heavenly lift, that only heroin can give. The heroin rushed through my nose, sinuses, face, and head all at once; then, as quickly as a burst of wind settled my body into a mood of serenity.

"Don't be f... nodding! When, I can't find a vein!" I heard her yelling, which brought me out of my stay of bliss.

"Sheee," the workers will hear you yelling."

"I don't care; just find us some place to stay!"

I sniffled a few times, rubbed my nose scratched my genitals and turned to Mimi who was having an agonizing time getting off. She was bleeding from her arms and legs where she'd previously tried to find a vein. I took the works from her and told her to stand up.

"Stick your finger in your mouth, honey, and blow," I said contented with the feeling of opiate as it made devoted love me.

Mimi knew the drill and stuck her thumb into her mouth, closed it, took a deep breath and blew her cheeks into a Dizzy Gillespie face, which caused her jugular vein to pop up on the side of her neck. However, just as I was about to tap the needle into it she lost her breath and we had to begin again.

"Do it again," I said. "Yeah honey, hold it right there, yeah right there." I gentle tapped the needle into her jugular and instantaneously blood popped up into the syringe; and I slowly shot the heroin within it.

Now that we were both high, I explained to Mimi that we'd be living with Diane, and why A.C. had a changed of mind. She'd never met Diane but had heard of her street toughness and didn't want to go anywhere near her, but had no better option.

When we exit the room one of the crewmembers, whom I thought was a bit old to be lifting furniture was standing in the hall wearing a blue khaki jumpsuit and holding a notepad, which he passed to Mimi with a hand cracked from hard work. After calling a cab and the phone company to have the phone line disconnected, we waited downstairs, in the foyer, for the cab to arrive.

It was early June and already the weather was as hot and sticky as August. When the cab arrived, we packed our few boxes into its trunk and upon the back seat. It was a tight fit for Mimi and me to sit, but we managed to squeeze in. When the cab pulled away from the curb and drove off beneath the huge trees, which lined Varndale Street on either side; Mimi dare not look back for fear she'd break in to tears.

I didn't care too much about leaving Brookline; nevertheless, I felt dispirited for both Mimi and Shanwda. Mimi did have a child and what better place to rear her than Brookline. Since it was around 2:00 p.m., we stopped at Shanwda's school and took her out an hour early. I switched from the back seat to the front seat to make room for her to be with her mother.

I had to push my heart back into my chest when I saw Diane's new Honda parked in front of her building when our cab slowed to a stop behind it. I looked at my watch, the only piece of jewelry I hadn't sold yet. It was 2:15 p.m. However, Diane wasn't supposed to be home until four.

From her second floor apartment window, Diane saw us getting out of the cab and already had her apartment door opened for us. With the cabby trailing behind us with a bunch of clothes hanging on hangers; she greeted us with a broad Mr. Ed smile—all teeth. After we had placed our things down, on the shinny hardwood floor, she gave the three of us a teddy-bear hug, a kiss on the cheeks, and a joyful hello.

"And what's your name, honey?" Diane said looking down at Shawnda, as I paid the cabby.

"Shawnda," she answered, childlike, smiling up at Diane.

"Oh, that's such a beautiful name," Diane said, shutting the door behind the cabdriver. Shawnda wasn't at all a shy child, thus, she answered. "Do you know what Shawnda means?"

"No honey, what does it mean?"

"It means 'gold' in Indian."

"Yes, yes, it does sound Native American. And you must be Mimi?"

"Yes," Mimi answered suitably.

Diane and Mimi were about the same height about five, four. Diane was brown-skinned, attractive, and perhaps in her forties. However, she'd been using drugs before I've known her some seventeen years. Yet she still held on to her nice-looks and well-stacked body. Not only was she shaped well, but body toned, too. Yet there was something about her that just didn't turn me on to sexually.

I gave Diane our weekly rent and no sooner had I done so she scooted out the apartment. Nevertheless, not before telling us that she'd cleaned off a shelf in the refrigerator and a space in the cabinet for our things.

We didn't have enough space in our bedroom to store our few belonging, so we had to leave a lot of things in their boxes.

Shawnda now going on nine and a little too old to sleep with us, slept on the floor in her sleeping bag that we'd already bought for her upcoming summer camping trip. However, we still had to come up with six-hundred dollars, for her six-weeks camping trip. I left Mimi and Shawnda for a moment and went out to the variety store on Shawmut Avenue to purchase a few things for snack. Latter we'd eat supper at "the church" on Shawmut. Upon returning to the apartment, Mimi and Shawnda were in the kitchen putting up some of the other things, like a few pots and pans we'd brought with us.

"Sheee," Mimi said to me as I placed the two bags of grocery on the round kitchen table. "Diane's upstairs in her room," she whispered, while Shawnda peeked into the bags looking for the pop sickle I'd promised to buy her. She was a petite child but an immense eater and gained not a pound.

"I know," I whispered; "I saw the car."

"Why are you all whispering?" Shawnda asked, as she brought out the six-packed of pop sickles.

"Put those pop sickles in the refrigerator until after your supper," Mimi uttered.

Both Mimi and I knew full well, from experience that Diane had taken the money I'd given her for rent and had gone out to buy some cocaine. Though she was on the methadone program for her heroin addiction and working full-time, five days a week, didn't stop her from being strung out on coke or a speed-balls in the evenings and almost all day on the weekend.

Methadone has its advantages, but also its disadvantages. One of the advantages is that an addict who is truly committee to his methadone programs, and serious about getting his life in order, can do so. It enabled him to hold down a job, take care of himself, rare a family. The disadvantage is that methadone is highly addicted, more addicted than heroin.

Addicts who are unwilling to change their addicted behaviors and play their methadone program for methadone, feel that when they're on methadone it give them the go ahead to began experiencing with other type of drugs along with the continually use of heroin. As long as they're on the methadone program, they don't have to worry about being sick. They use the program for a safety net, not for its wellness; thus, blowing all changes of presenting their life in order. Many of the methadone patients on those programs are given as much as 100 mg. or more on a daily basis, seven days a week; that's a lot of methadone.

What the junkie will do, with his takeout, is drink half, and sells the other half, on the street, for a dollar a milligram, making some three hundred dollars per week, "free money" as it is called among those on the program. Ninety nine point nine percent of the methadone sold on the street diluted with water so that the junkie might make more cash. From the money, they buy heroin, or coke, or pills, or some other get high. Hence, never getting well, thus walking the streets looking like the bogeymen. Even so, not all addicts on the math programs sell their meth; they took it and started new lives, some took it and took very good care of themselves, their wife and children. The kids, especially the boys of addicts' parents who got their lives back in order, by any wellness, or therapeutic programs, are just so happy having their parent at home working and building a family.

When Shawnda returned home from summer camp in late August, we were still living with Diane, though we had hoped to move by the time of her return. However, regress instead of progress seems to be the addict's forte. Things were not working out for us. Mimi and I were as low down as we could be, and we were out there in all sort of weather flatfoot hustling—I breaking into people's home, and she turning tricks.

Moreover, there was always some kind of drama going on in the house. When Mimi and I weren't raving at each other then, it was Diane and I. Every night, every night, after Diane shot up her money on coke she became a real b... the coke had left her edgy and extreme. The side effect from the coke paraded through her thick, brown body like, Louisiana red ants on a warpath. She couldn't remain still for a second. Therefore, every night she ranted and raved at Mimi for no a parent reason. She ranted until she shook off the red ants jitter and her methadone kicked in again, now sending her into a languor; whereby she went to her room; then to bed.

Because Diane had been in the street and in prison, and Mimi had not been in prison, she was dreadfully afraid of Diane and never uttered a word whatsoever to Diane insulting her. Therefore, I'd pick up Mimi's beef, and Diane and I would go at it, yelling at each other like two lunatics. We were never physical but we were as verbal as lighting and thunder.

That November afternoon, while Diane was still at work, I asked Mimi how she felt. For a few days ago, she'd gotten off in her middle finger. Pushing the needle in too deep had caused her to hit the bone, causing her finger and right hand to swell. The dope held down her fever some, but she kept getting hotter and hotter and sicker and sicker. It wasn't until her hand had swelled to twice its normal size did we make the decision to go to New England Medical Center.

First we needed to get off, not that we needed a shot but because we were junkies. In addition, we wanted to be straight if we were to spend the whole night in the hospital's emergency room. That day we had some money. Both Mimi and I had some luck in the hustling world; so we'd bought two quarters of scramble egg, or heroin that couldn't stand another cut, meaning that the dope in the street was still weak. It wasn't that good, but did well on the street for that was the only thing out there.

After getting off, we walked Shawnda—no, we never got off in front of Shawna—across the street, to the Lenox Street Housing Project, to her babysitter. Then, headed for Northampton "T" station and took the "EL," or elevated train to China Town. At China Town "T" station, we walked up the stairs and down Washington Street into the heart of the Combat-Zone towards the hospital. Washington Street was blazing with neon lightings, and the strip joints were profiting from the tongue-hanging perverts whom frequent them.

The whore promenade up and down Beach Street and Harrison Avenue luring tricks to their nest for sex while, the drug dealers shifted from allies to streets peddling their poison. The pimps, forever grabbing at their crotch as a sign of coolness, stood on the sidewalk. Most of them were dressed Disco, Gil Scott-Heron Afro hairstyles. Others wore their hair in finger waves processes while others wore their hair as Nat King Cole wore his. On their feet were colorful disco shoes, which complimented their bell-bottom polyester slacks, and Sammy Davis shirts—the ones with the large collars.

The doctors who examined Mimi at New England Medical Center emergency room were young and just outright rude; what an ignominy, the way they treated her. They verbally insulted her for being an addict; and that it was her own fault for her infected finger. They cared not that her temperature was 103 and that she was severely sick. When I asked them to stop treating her that way, they went right own with their verbal insinuations. I so much wanted to approach the three of them, right there at Mimi's bed and beat them in to the floor.

Yet, I knew that if I touched just one of those cowards jail awaited me. Moreover, right now my concern, Mimi and Shawnda. Nevertheless, I swore, then, that if I were to cross paths with any of the doctors again, I would assert my insults upon them the street way. I can just imagine how many other sick persons those doctors insulted in the course of their practice. They were ugly!

Because of her infected finger and fever, they admitted her into the hospital. However, because she had no health insurance, the New England Medical Center refused outright to treat her; another act of ill-mannered treatment this time by the hospital administration.

That night, around 10:00 p.m. with a light snow falling and dissolving as it gently fell on the pavement, Mimi was place in an ambulance, with me at her side, and transferred to the Shattuck State Hospital in Jamaica Plain.

At Shattuck, the doctor placed her in a single room and put her to bed, where the doctor and nurses treated her with respect. After examining her, the young doctor with blue-black hair wearing a paper-white doctor's jackets and sporting what looked like a Caribbean suntan on his boyish face, placed her on antibiotics for the infected finger and methadone to maintain her addiction. I left the hospital assuring her that all would be all right and guaranteed her that me and Shawna would visit her every evening until her discharged. Being that Mimi had also hit the bone in her finger her doctors felt for sure that she'd be in the hospital for at least six-weeks. In addition, for six-weeks Shawna and I visited her ever evening.

That Thanksgiving Shawnda and I had dinner with her at the hospital. Moreover, on Christmas Eve I even weaseled into her room a bottle of champagne and two shell glasses. I just couldn't see drinking champagne out of paper-cups or ordinary drinking glasses. For to do so, I felt, would ruin the taste of the champagne.

Many mornings, while Mimi was in the hospital, I woke up dope sick, yet I made sure that Shawnda went to school wearing clean clothes and her homework done, which she'd did with her mother on our visits. Shawnda was a highly bright and clever child and a quick learner, so she did well in school and learning came easy for her. At ten, she had spoke to me over the phone, at a time when I was in prison, about Buddha's Eight Paths of Wisdom, which she had read in one of my books at home. Moreover, she also thought that she knew it all at her age. Likewise, when she played games, like checkers, Pac Man ... or jump rope ... with either her friends or Mimi and me, she'd make up her own rules, in order to win the contest.

Mimi, unlike Marcia who remained a nurturing eye-on mother who made sure, even without me that the kids would go on to college. On the other hand, and sorry to say, but Mimi was a full-blown junkie, hooker/prostitute, stripper and street smart; thus, Mimzee nor I was in any shape to shape Shawnda into an established person. For sure enough, later on in her young life Shawna became a trouble child, who became a ward of the state, end up in court and further on went into forester care. Even so, her brightness got her through college with an Associate Degree; and when I saw her three years ago, she was living in Atlanta doing very well.

Pam, my daughter, didn't do much better in her young life, either; for in the 1980s she too got hooked on heroin and begun shoplifting to support her habit. She used dope for years, until she took an overdose and woke up in the hospital. That and a year or so in county for shoplifting changed Pam's life. She went into detox and then into a long-term therapeutic drug resident. Finishing the program, after a year, she went on to manage a halfway house for homeless mothers and their young children. The mothers had once been addicted to heroin … and stayed, there in drug treatment, working daily, until they completed the program or received affordable housing through HUD. Pam is doing well today, and been cleaned since August 2002.

My fear wasn't whether or not I could look out for Shawnda, but would I get arrested before Mimi got discharged. For I was still an addict, still had to support my jones, pay rent, buy food, and do laundry; and on occasions bring Mimi things like magazine, toiletries, and sometime a meal, from Howard Johnson, which was across the street from the hospital. All this took money, and that meant that I had to get out there in the street and do my thing while Shawnda was in school. If I wasn't dope sick, I'd go out around 11:00 a.m., and If I was dope sick, I'd leave the house right behind Shawnda, around 8:00 a.m. to do break ins.

It took me about two hours to do my hustle. Sometimes I made enough money to last for days, and sometime I only made enough money to last a day, if that. However, as Macbeth put it, "Life's but a walking shadow to a poor player that struts and frets his hour upon the stage … " It was easy for me to spend twelve hundred dollars a week just on my habit, never mind Mimi's habit. Heroin was then forty dollars a bag, because of the shortage and weakness of the dope. The only thing on the market was scramble eggs, or dope cut below par.

I was out there in the street, mostly every day, working my trade without taking an arrest the whole time Mimzee was in the hospital. In addition, yeah, because of my heroin addiction, B&E was my vocation—and I did make a career of it. God truly love me, because I'm certain that if it wasn't for Him, Diane would have cast Shawnda into the arms of the Social Services Department. Shawnda was better off with me.

Two weeks before Mimi was to be discharge we received good news that her name had finally rose to the top of the Boston Housing waiting list. She'd gotten an apartment in Cathedral Housing Project in the South End. Since she was still hospitalized, I as her other half took care of the housing issues.

The housing manager, who was a large woman with a social worker's kindness, explained to me that the apartment was on the tenth floor at twenty-five Monsignor Reynolds Way, and wouldn't be ready for inhabitant for at least four to five weeks. She said that they still had to paint the two bedrooms apartment and fix the plumbing in the bathroom.

"Oh no, no, please, we can't wait that long!" I uttered. "We just got to get out of where we're staying. There are just too much frictions going on between us and the woman we're rent from. We need to move as soon as Meredith is discharged from the hospital; and that's within the next two weeks. Moreover, don't worry about the painting, you supply the supplies, and I'll paint the place. You just work on getting the plumbing done within the next two weeks."

The amiable manager, who had dealt many times with people down on their luck, understood our plight and agreed to work with us. She then gave me the keys to the apartment and off I went. "Oh," she said as I near the exit door, "the elevator may not be working; then, again it's hardly ever working. Now we're having a new elevator placed in the building and that should be ready next week.

I really didn't care if I had to walk up the tenth flights of stairs, as long as we could finally free ourselves of Diane's madness. Even so, the day we moved out of Diane's apartment in early '83, she and I, again, became the best of friends. Just as she had greeted us at her apartment door, the day we move in, is the self same why she treated us upon our moving out full of warmth. In late 1990, Diane died in the hospital of HIV.

Well, it just happened that the old telephone booth scaled elevated was working. And as I stood there waiting for it to decent from its gory where-about, I felt a rage of disgust come over me. We were at our lowest denominator. I could hear the grunting and squeals of the elevator as it made its way down, mourning like a person in dying pain.

The once yellow-glazed cinder block walls in the hallways had turned a slimy, moldy brown. It seemed as though the floor hadn't been swept or mopped in eons. The smell of urine and feces and other foul odors filled the air. The aluminum mailboxes, which lined the wall across from the elevator, were in a calamity. Their shutter were either hanging, or going all together, making them unusable.

The primitive elevator came to a rugged stop, while its dark-blue doors opened at a snail's pace. I wasn't at all surprise to find the elevator as filthy as the hallways. This would not be a problem, for I could keep the elevator clean by cleaning it myself. I got off the elevator on the top floor, the tenth floor and wow, the hallways was Ritz Carlton clean compared to what I'd seen on the first floor; and with very little work I could keep the floor clean. Before entering the apartment, I examined the two dead-bolt locks on the scratched navy-gray painted metal door and metal doorframe, to see just how capable they were against thieves. They were both solid, but not thieve proofed. What locks are? Nevertheless, I did feel good about the safety of the locks, door and the doorframe.

I entered the apartment and strolled through the small place. Yes as the house manager warned, it certainly needed a great deal of work. Every room had wallpaper or paint peeling from its walls, and needed stripping before painting. I had about two weeks to get the house in shape. I thought I'd first do Shawnda's bedroom, the kitchen, bedroom, and so on. To my amazement from one of the windows in Shawdna's bedroom, I could see clearly the Boston Harbor. Moreover, with my World War II binocular I'll be able to see the tall ships when they sail into the harbor.

Mimi was discharged a day before New Year. In addition, that night we went out partying and had a ball. One week later, we moved into the Cathedral Housing Project, at that time, the toughest housing projects in the city of Boston. The only room not finished when we moved in was the living room. However, before I could complete it and while the apartment still had that scent of paint and freshness—the Boston police arrested me for braking and entrancing in the daytime to committee a felony and possession of burglary tools.

Mimi began using again the first day she was discharged from the hospital; so, we definitely couldn't afford the outrageous, fifty thousand dollar, bail place on me by the court. Thus, the court sent me to the Charles Street Jail to await trial. Now it was Mimi's turn to visit me and, she treated me as I'd treated her when she was hospitalized. She visited me while I lay in the county jail; and again when I was in prison serving six to ten years for my offences.

After serving two and a half years in different prisons within the system, Plymouth Forestry Camp, a minimum-security facility, classification board sent me to Hillside Pre-release Center at Columbus Avenue and Jackson Square. Yes, right there in pre-release, I picked up again and within five-months, the center busted me for having a dirty, heroin urine. Thus, sent me back behind the walls to serve the remaining of my sentence, and that ended the relationship between Mimi and me.

In 1989, on an exceptional gentle windy day in June a yellow sun dominate a clear blue sky and the fresh scent of recently summer-mowed grass. I walked out prison, discharged, after completing my sentence at Shirley medium security prison. There, at the prison one of my main man—or best friend, Stanley Jones, waited for me in the prison's parking lot in his newly purchased Cadillac.

Stanley first drove me to a bank in the town of Shirley where I cashed my check for thirty-five hundred dollars. I gave Stanley a handsome "$gaper," for picking me up, as we drove down Route 2, talking about ways for me to stay clean and free of drugs. Stanley had not picked up in fifteen years, and was still director of Yesterday Today and Tomorrow drug programs, now both a in prison and on the street program.

Nevertheless, no sooner had he dropped me off at my sister's house in Mattapan, I rushed to the back of the house to where my sister had left a set of keys hidden in the Bar-B-Q coal bend. Once in the house I went straight to the basement, and that was to hide my money. I peeled five twenty dollars bills from the stack of money and hide the rest behind a large, lengthy wooden table used for laundering.

I then darted out the front door and fleetly walked up the street to Blue Hill Avenue where I crabbed a cab, and headed to Dudley Square. I wanted a fix of heroin so bad that I was hyperventilating, and felt as if I were going to swallow my anxiety and choke to death on it. My compulsion was on a collision course with heroin and there was nothing I could do to stop the crash, for Satan was driving my car, I felt captivated. I would have walked on a bed of sizzling coal for a bag of pee-funk.

On Washington Street at Dudley Square, I bumped in to an OG, or a hustler, from the old school, standing near the liquor store/fish market. "Damn baby!" when you get out?" Pop Crecy uttered when I approach him, giving me one of those big friendly bear hug.

"I just got out and need a bag!" I said during our friendly hug.

"Yeah, I been there before and I'll be there again, but right now I got what you want—and it's good," the once golden boy of the pimp game assured me.

Now in his early sixties, Pop Crecy was touting heroin for some young dope, dealing tug who thought himself a gangster. The two of us moseyed around the corner into an ally were the still handsome, well dressed, and former pimp served me.

I stayed in the ally and gently tore opened the bag poured the heroin onto the back of my right hand, and in one snort, snorted up the tiny amount of heroin. By the time I walked back to where Pop Crecy was standing, the dope had already hit me and the high was just where I wanted to be, where no one knew I was high but me. I didn't want to meet my sister nodding and scratching.

TWENTY

BOSTON UNIVERSITY and MY MENTOR

It took me three months to fine employment, and then went to work as a counselor at the Pine Street Inn—a shelter for the homeless. I was already volunteering at the Howard Thurman Center at Boston University as an assistant to the late legendary, Emeritus Dean George K. MaKechnie who spent over seventy years at BU, on campus and in the community at large. In addition, whom I'm proud to say was my mentor and very good friend, as well.

I had again been hooked on heroin, during the three months since my release, but had since gotten on a methadone program, which allowed me to keep going thinking; maybe something good might come out of it.

I first met Dean George, as they called him at BU and across the world, at Norfolk State Prison in the late '80s. He, through BU, along with the Norfolk's Chaplains team sprouted the Howard Thurman "Listening Room" at Norfolk prison. Moreover, since I was a lector in the Catholic Church and a real bright fellow, I became part of the Thurman team there. The more I heard of the late Howard Thurman the more I wanted to know the man, "Shall I be good because of some reward," Dr. Thurman exclaimed, "because the virtuous act pays dividends? No! I shall be good because it is good."

Howard Thurman was dean of Marsh Chapel at Boston University from 1953 until his retirement in 1965. He was the first black person appointed to an administrative deanship in a predominantly white university anywhere in the United States. He was dean emeritus at the time of his death in 1981.

In his retirement, Dean George made sure that his friend's legacy lived on. Thus, he begun the Howard Thurman Center at BU and became its director. He loved his work and enjoyed movement. Then at eighty-six, he had much more energy and motivation than some men did in their forties, which kept him sparkling upon the stage. Dean George didn't have a Television in his home, said they were "polluted." His preferences was reading the daily newspapers and listing to the radio. Dean George also preferred not to eat before a major speech; and had no problem eating a dinner for breakfast; breakfast could be what he'd eaten for supper. He was made of steel, yet he was soft as down in his work, a kind and goodhearted men.

The man had style as well; and always neatly dressed in his three-piece pin stripe suites—impeccably fitting him. He even had a mini bounce in his steps. I loved that man! Dean George's aim was to bring Thurman's concept into prisons, jails, and pre-releases centers. Therefore, a Howard Thurman Listening Room was, set up in one of the chaplains' rooms, at Norfolk. Where prisoners, whether Muslim, Catholic, Protestant, or non denominational could drop by during the day time hours, if they wanted to, to read Thurman's many books and listen to his many tapes on mysticism, love of God, love of self, love of neighbor, and on "common ground."

"*Howard,*" his wife, the late Sue Bailey Thurman wrote, "would have the individual seek the solution by searching from within the self, until the inner becomes the outer, and the heart a swinging door. He spent his life in the high cause of Love's magnificence."

I felled in love with Howard's "Love's magnificence" at once, because peace and love was my unvarying self-study. I knew no matter my behavior that I'd never find peace outside myself or out there in the mundane world. There were a different between the Self and the mundane. I had been there many times while in meditation, on the threshold, the Centre, which separates the one from the other.

What impressed Dean George about me, is when I stood before the podium at one of our yearly Catholic Church banquets at Norfolk prison, and reflected, from memory, some pages from one of Howard's books, *Jesus and the Disinherited.* He was so overwhelm with my presentation, that from that day onward we became friends.

When discharge from up my sentence June 1989, I went to BU to see Dean George at the Howard Thurman Center, then on Deerfield Street, where he invited me to work with him, at the center, as a part-time volunteer. He knew that I had a drug problem before I went to prison, but didn't know that I'd been hooked since my release.

Before I knew it Dean George was ushering me about the campus visiting this building and than that building in order for me to see, learn, and meet faculty and students. I'm quite sure now that he had bigger plans for me at the university. In fact, in his book, *70 Stories About Boston University 1923 – 1993,* He signed his book over to me as: "To Oren with high hopes," Dean George. Dean George really wished the best for me and wanted me to attend the university. However, self-education had its place in society. Hadn't I proved it by being at BU, one of the chief universities in the country?

I had many proud moments at BU with having Dean George as friend and mentor, chatting with students, going to President John R. Silber's party, speak at Sergent College of Allied Health Professions at Boston University where Dean George was once dean. On occasions, some of those students and I would meet in the Howard Thurman Listening Room in the basement at Marsh Chapel to discuss substance abuse and human growth.

I also spoke to some out of town scholars at George Sherman Union Hill. Dean George wanted me to lecture them on "real life's issues." In other words, he wanted me to bring them down to the common, man level of understanding, so that they might at least climb off their high horses for a day. Everyone I met at BU, through Dean George, knew that I'd been in prison and that I'd met my mentor there. Moreover, at once they liked me because the Dean constantly spoke well in my behalf.

My greatest honor, through BU, came when I spoke at the historical African Meeting House where the Howard Thurman Center was celebrating its Martin Luther King Jr. birthday, with compliment to Howard Thurman. As I climbed the three small steps to the tiny stage and approached the podium to speak on Howard's legacy. My thoughts rushed in, to remind me that I was about to speak to a standing crowd only at the famous, African Meeting House. That was once part of the Underground Railroad and where the Herculean abolitionists, and Frederick Douglas along with the fearless, Williams Lloyd Garrison, spoke on issues to end slavery. I mean, I had made it to a place in my life where under Dean George support I could have done well. However, my life still had its quest. "I hated safety and wanted no path that did not have its snares," wrote Saint Augustine, in his quest for the closeness of God.

On November 15, 1993, two weeks away from my fiftieth birthday, I got busted, in a house break and charged with home invasion, breaking and entrancing in the daytime and an added on—attempted murder. After I'd already broken into the house and stripped it of its cash and jewelry, the occupants were returning home as I exited their apartment. At first, the three persons were puzzled for an instant, as to what I'm doing coming out of their apartment. You know, like one of those head-scratching questions. The woman with yellow skin and a friendly round face even gave me an ample smile.

Nevertheless, the man with an accent quickly figured it out and snapped, "Why you coming out my apartment?" With the swiftness of a martial artist, he grabbed my left wrist, as I tried squeezing through him, the woman, and a young man, in his late teens, coming up the tiny stairwell. When he did this, I reached into the pocket of my, Lacoste, jacket, placed my thumb on the edge of the smooth steel blade, and when I exit with the knife, my thumb quickly slide the blade opened which I used to make a small cut across the victim left chest. If I didn't know what I was doing and had stabbed him it the chest instead of a small cut, I would have killed him.

I had no intent of killing him or causing him great harm. However, let us suppose some thing would have gone wrong, like the victim falling on the knife. ... I just wanted him to let go of my wrist, which he did. With my wrist free and the knife back in my pocket, I fleeted down the stairs, out the glass door, and onto the street. I darted toward my car parked just around the corner. I hurriedly climbed in, shut and locked the door, and keyed the car in to action.

However, before I could pulled the car out of its tight parking space, my victim was banging on the driver's window, screaming, and trying to smashed the window with his bloody fists. I finally got the car freed and speed away with my victims, the woman, and the young man yelling and chasing me in the middle of the street. I lost them as I made my way through the small street. I then drove to Dudley Square and bought four bags of dope. All the time thinking that perhaps, the victims hadn't gotten my license plate number. I thought of driving over to my buddy, Johnny Drayton, house and hang out there—then later call my sister to see if the cops had been by. I felt as if my mind were running ahead of me like one of those manual rabbits at a dog track. However, if they had gotten my plate number and reported it I'd be a wanted man. I jumped the idea of going to Johnny's and took the chance of going home, hoping the cops wouldn't show.

I said hello to Laura, who was sitting in the family room, in her favorite chair, watching her favorite television show, *Murder She Wrote,* as I made my way up the stairs to my comfortable loft. My sister was a quiet person, and rather be along with her thoughts. However, those were just her wishes. For years, she forever had family members living with her who was down on their luck.

If it wasn't me she argued with, then it was her son. At one time, we were all living together, where my dear sister gave up her own room to one of her granddaughters, and slept on the couch in the living room. Though Laura mood in the house could be ice cold at times, she was extremely kind and the backbone of the family. She would not let us complain about our hard times or our disorders. Her thing was, "get your life in order and get the hell out!" Than, she'd fuss until we did move out. In our disagreements, and we had our share of them, I always told her that my love for her was everlasting.

Up in my loft I cooked up the four-bags of dope, got off and instantaneously I felt the rush that sent me into a nod. I was high but not relax, and the heroin just so, so. I felt doomed. After washing the works, I stuffed them into a sock, and stashed them in the back of my sock's drawer. As I turned on the television, I thought I heard the doorbell down stairs ring, but brushed it off as a sound coming from the TV. Again, it went "ding-dong, ding-dong."

Damn! The cops! I froze where I stood, at the dresser drawers, and lifted my ears as thieves and animals do, so that I might clearly hear who rang the doorbell. I heard my sister open the door; then, heard a man voice asked? "Who own the car in the drive way?"

"It's my brother's car."

"Damn! The cops," I whispered. Then like a rat, looking for a way out, I quickly scuttled down the stairs and into the kitchen where I opened the back door to steal my way to freedom.

However, a cop standing on the lawn near the back door saw me, and immediately I closed and locked the door. "There's a back door! There's back door!" he yelled out." *The house surrounded,* I thought. As I turned from the door feeling trapped, I spotted the towering, pencil shaped cop entering the kitchen with Laura following behind. She was short in body and I didn't see her, behind the tall and pencil shape police officer until she took a chair, at the kitchen table.

"Is that your car in the parking lot?" the cop asked with polished manner.

"Yes." I couldn't lie, for my sister had already said so. In addition, one thing she wouldn't do, even for her own children, is lie for us.

"Well," said the pencil looking cop, "there are a couple of detectives want to ask you a few questions at the Massachusetts General Hospital, and you should come with us."

"Why do they want to see me?" I asked imperatively, trying to take control of the situation, yet, trying to use words that wouldn't frighten Laura, for she was easily frighten.

"Oh, you're not under arrest, they just want to talk."

"Why?"

"They didn't say, they just asked us to pick you up and take you to Massachusetts General Hospital."

"If I'm not under arrest, then, I'm not going," I said arrogantly.

"Look, Oren, you're not under arrest, I want even handcuff you, but you will come with us."

Laura looked at me and asked in a tender voice, "Oren, what have you done?" I didn't answer.

"Go with them and see what they want with you at the hospital," she said. "He said you're not under arrest, it might be about nothing."

"You're going to need your shoes and a jacket," the tall lanky pleasant looking, well manner cop said.

In my haste to flee, I'd forgotten that I had no shoes on. When I moved to go upstairs the cop said, "I'll get them. Where's your room?"

"Up stair," Laura said." The cop turned, went up stairs, while his buddy, who stood in the nearby hallway watching the whole thing kept watch. The cop returned carrying; both my desert booths and Lacoste win breaker, Safari jacket. However, for a November night the weather was quite warm.

At MGH the two cops, pencil cop and his gargantuan looking partner, hustled me into the emergency room area, where two plain-clothes detectives stood near the bed of an Asian male in his late twenty, with his chest wrapped in gauze. As soon as the bedded person saw me, he raised himself on his right elbow, and those once beaded eyes of his grew larger and larger; then, he screamed, "That him! "That him! That him, him, that ... "

He continued yelling as he now tried getting out of bed to chew me up. However, one of the detectives, dressed in polyester, placed a mild hand on the victim bare shoulder and this was enough to restrain him.

"That him! I can tell by his jacket with the alligator."

I could see that he was no punk, and was quite pleased that I'd gotten to my car before he'd gotten to me. At the hospital, the woman was the only person, of the three, that could not identify me. I guess she looked upon my face and saw only kindness. "What?" I am a kind person; however, heroin was ugly, very, very ugly. Nevertheless, the victim had no contradiction in recognizing me.

When back in prison, servicing 10 to 15 years in prison, I went back to my studies and my prayers, and believed deeply that this time would certainly by my last time a dope fiend and a prison itinerary. It was time for me to grow up not some innocent person. In addition, the only one, that could destroy the monkey on my back, was I. Not AA, or NA or Twelve Steps; no, it had to be me. Furthermore, I know longer believe that addiction was a disease, but rather a compulsion behavior problem. The first thing I gave up on believing is that—"once a junky always a junky." That's so far from being the truth. God gave us the Ten Commandments to follow, not twelve Steps. Nevertheless, I'm not saying that addicts should give up these drug programs. If these programs work for you than, please continue attending them. They didn't work for me.

"Once a junky always a junky" isn't in my thinking any longer. However, AA and NA believe it so. Instead of the addicts in these programs killing the monkey on their back they continue to keep it alive by forever introducing themselves at substance abuse meeting as, "hi I'm Joe Blow, and I'm a heroin addict." When the addict is in recovery, he should stop believing that he will be a junky for the rest of his life no matter how long he's been clean. The Addicts in recovery are afraid to let go of, "and I'm a junky." He keeps to "I'm an addict and my addiction a disease.

While in prison, I involved myself in the Catholic Church and study, and took two corresponding courses, with the Writer's Digest University, paying for them out of my own prison canteen fund. The first course was in "Writing and Selling Short Stories" and the latter, the "Elements of Effective Writing, and received a certificate in both. For the next eight-years and two months, I busy my time with education and my work in the church.

By early year 2000, I'd finished both courses, and had already gotten some eighteen rejection slips from editors; with most coming from periodicals that I'd submitted some of my articles. Like some beginners, before horning our writing craft, we thrust forward taking our chances and scattering our crude writings around to different magazines. We really believed that our articles were good enough even for: *Harper's, The New Yorker, Maxim,* and so on. Of all the periodicals I submitted to Ebony and *Maxim* were the only two that, while rejecting me, gave me hope to keep writing. Their personal comments boost my muse and placed confidence in my pen.

In that same year, 2000, while still in prison, I began writing for *Spare Change Newspaper,* a street newspaper published bimonthly in a church's basement, in the city of Cambridge. My first article to the paper was on John Salvi, "Maximum Security Haircut," who was serving a life sentence for the brutal Brookline, Massachusetts abortion clinic murders of Shannon Lowey and Lee Nichols.

It was then the winter of 1996, the day sub-zero, and ice and snow covered the ground when Salvi and I met. We were both at Concord Prison, he in segregation confinement and I in the main population working as lead barber in the prison's barbershop, as one of four barbers. On a Saturday afternoon after lunch, on my day off, Captain Murphy sent me to the hole, or Department-9, to cut John Salvi's hair.

When the heavy steel door to Department-9 banged shut behind me, I felt entombed. The lighting was dull and yellowish and the atmosphere gory. This was a place of violent, where even the air had become violent and fought with the smelt of human musk and un-washed toilets. Salvi was a little person with brown hair, shinny dark eyes, weighing no more than a hundred and twenty pounds. In addition, his face was chalked white from months in the hole.

The guard open Salvi's barred door and sat, him still handcuffed, in one of those old captain's chairs, which look like it had been around the prison for many years. It was hard for my customer to sit in the old antique chair, for the guard had handcuffed him with his hands behind his back.

"How would you like me to cut your hair?" I kindly said. *Be cool with this cat and watch his body language in case he snaps,* I thought. Not knowing how to read signs and body language could get a prisoner killed. Most times when leaving my cell, I'd whisper to myself, "Watch it."

"Just cut a little off the back," he answered in a voice that seemed as if it were coming from far-off. The dude was unpredictable and weird thus the guard stood close. Salvi committed suicide a couple years later at Walpole. The administration claimed he'd hung himself. However, it's still a question among prisoners, whether he killed himself or not?

TWENTY-ONE

WALKING TALL

I couldn't have asked for a better day to end prison life after serving eight years and two months. It was an exceptional late January day, 2002—one of those, autumn/spring blended days. Leaving prison, a homeless person, dressed only in a grey sweatshirt and a pair of dungaree, didn't faze me a bit—I was walking tall—felt free. In fact never before had I felt so physically and mentally powerful and never so sure of myself. For the first time in my life, I was coming out of prison with no desire to used heroin, whatsoever. I had prepared myself well for that moment in my life. I was ready to tackle my adversaries, my anxieties and compulsions.

I was now strong enough and grown enough to diss heroin, to now treat it like the loser, a no, no. I felt great defeating the devil. I no longer allowed my anxiety to run wild—I took control and positioned anxiety to my back, kept it in check with constant prayer. God is the only substance abuse program I need to finish my journey.

Yes, I'd be homeless but I had a plan. I'd saved my money over the years, in the joint, and came out with a good chunk of it. Thus, I rented a room, at the YMCA on Huntington Avenue, for forty-five dollars a day, right next door to Northeastern University. The "Y" had a ten days occupant lodge policy. That meant I had ten days to find a room or a place to live. Every morning after eating a healthy breakfast at Fred's Pizza, just across the street from the "Y," I went out looking for a place to live, but failed each time. No one wanted to rent to me, an ex-offender, even after offering six-months rent in advance. Moreover, oh, quite so quickly, my ten days were up, thus, I met with the manager of the "Y" asking him to give me three more days. He agreed. Yet, after three days, I still hadn't found anything. The last thing I wanted to do was go into a shelter. However, if I had to do it until I found a place to live, I would.

However, I'd no other choice but to go to a homeless shelter, most likely, the Pine Street Inn. The setback would not rob me of my strength and mind to succeed. I just wasn't going back to prison, nor was I going to pick up heroin ever again. Heroin was the past, where my life had passed through its thunders, into calmness. Though my canoe and I had gone through *hell* where my body had gotten scared up, cut up, and beat up both externally and internally on the sharp rocks in path of the rapids. Even so, I had won; I had peddled and zigzag like a combatant through the rapids of fire, demons, and fiends; Dante and Vigil, imps, Sodom and Gomorrah, prison, drugs—and Heroin, Satan himself! I'd been to hell and rise from it with Vigil as he made his way up from the depth of inferno.

My last morning at the "Y" as I was checking out and on my way to Pine Street Inn shelter for the homeless, the desk phone rang and the manager picked it up, listened; and then, passed it to me. "It's your sister," he said, giving me a curious look.

On the other end of the phone was my sister, Laura sounding bright and full of get-up-and-go inviting me to come live with her. God had tested my faith, and though I hadn't gotten a place to live, I trusted Him enough not to picked up. Therefore, when Laura called just at the moment when I was homeless it was a God sent. I was so thankful, now that I'd a home to live and work on my book; get involved in community issues, as a community activist … all from a comfortable, cozy and tidy home. That same sister, in 1993, had seen me go away that November night with the well-mannered penciled shaped cop and his contemporaries. Laura was again placing her faith in me. All she wanted was to see me do well and beat heroin. My dear sister died in her sleep, April 11, 2008. Even so, she lived long enough to see me diss heroin.

While at Laura's, I jumped knee-deep into working as a community activities; and was soon involved with the Mattapan Community Development

Corporation, MCDC. I'd learned a lot about community development from the ground up while there. MCDC worked on most of the community issues in Mattapan, from after school programs to development homes for seniors, affordable housing and affordable condominiums for low and moderate working applicant. I got a birdied view of the ugly politics and its bureaucracy. It was a maze getting things done for the neighborhood, for it were politics as usually. As well, I worked for the Mattapan and Vicinity Task Force and there, chosen by its members to coordinate the Farmers Market issues.

Farmers Market is a supermarket in the Mattapan square area, that had been having a great deal of problems with Boston Inspectional Services Department, or ISD, and the community residents for multiple store violations: Toxic chemical stored with food, old and active mouse droppings in storerooms, meat and ice cream stored under unsafe temperature. The lunchroom where the employees took their breaks was mucky and resembled the pit of a slave-ship. The garbage dumpster outside, and a small area surrounding it constantly smelt of rotten food and urine, and that was a shame to Mattapan Square.

Most of the community residents wanted the market's owner to clean up the mess and stay in business, but there were those that wanted the market shutdown. Thus, the community leaders called a town hall meeting at Saint Angela Catholic Church, "on the hill," in Mattapan where more than two hundred people sat or stood in the churches auditorium. Sitting at long tables, at the front of the room were community residents and activists, the owner and manager of Farmers Market, the commissioner from ISD and his assistants. Present also were two members from the state's legislature.

Sitting in the back row listening to Representative Marie St. Fleur oratory on the deplorable condition of Farmers Market, my mind drifted off for a few minutes. Two weeks ago, I was in prison—tonight I'm setting in a community town hall meeting making comments on how to keep a store open and saved the jobs of a hundred pauper people who worked there. I came out of my mind drift, when Mr. Lopez, a prominent leader in the community, began speaking his voice domineering, almost intimidating. He wanted the market shutdown; "Pack up and get out!" he bellowed..

That started a fight between the pro and the con. People were trying to talk but someone else would cut in and it went on like that for a while. I wanted to speak and when I saw a slight opening, I stood up and in an imposing voice said, "Why not place the market owner on a probation period until he cleans up his act, and his store. The community residents and its activists can form a task force to work hand-in-hand with the market's owner to make sure he cleans it up." A loud applaud came roaring from the majority of the attendants in favor of my proposal. Before I could speak about the job that would be lost if the market closed, Mr. Lopez interjected.

"Yeah," he called out. "Yeah, yeah that's a good idea." The crowd was with my suggestion, and Mr. Lopez had to say something to take control of my idea and the meeting. Thus, he bided to run the Farmers Market probation period from his neighborhood community program, the MVTF, or the "Mattapan and Vicinity Task Force." Therefore, it went.

In a meeting at another time MVTF chose me coordinator for the "Sub-Committee for Farmers Market," I met with the market's owner on a daily basis, making sure that the owner corrected the violations ordered by ISD. In addition to other contentions placed on him by the community: refurbish and paint the employees' lunchroom, place new tables and chairs in it, add a microwave, and paint the stairway that led down to the meat-cutting room below. He had to make sure that his dumpster's area was fenced in, and free of filth and stink.

After six months of closely working with the market's owner, the Mayor's office and ISD I reported, back to the members at MVTF that Farmers Market had met both the ISD's health codes, and the community contentions. Therefore, the owner of the market and one hundred triumphantly employees went back to work. For helping to keep, the market open and saving a hundred jobs, I received MCDC "Outstanding Community Award," for the year 2004. When taking the coordinator's job to clean up Farmers Market, I told my son Darryl that I felt a new life developing in me. I have been clean since, November 15, 1993, when the cops took me from my sister's home … In addition, January 15, 2010, made it sixteen years since I last picked up! Thank you Jesus, I could not have done it without you! Since receiving the MCDC award in 2004, I since then, in 2007, received the SJCSPCA Stanley Jones Clean Slat Project Courage Award, both in Journalism and for the courage to change my past behavior and to stick it out.

Moreover, on the same night I received the SJCSPCA, I also received courage awards in Journalism, from both The Commonwealth of Massachusetts House of Representative and the City of Boston City Council. At the time,

I was writing for the *Spare Change Newspaper,* an affiliate of the North American Street Newspaper Association and working on my book. The Stanley Jones Clean Slate Program is the offspring of "Yesterday Today and Tomorrow," whom, today, work with substance abusers, in and out of prison, and with the ex-offenders, by helping them upon their release from prison find jobs and housings.

Even so, at the time of my receiving, the courage awards my life was in crisis and I'd see just how much courage I really had. For I'd just received a 30 day notice of eviction from my landlord in the South End, where I was then staying. I had a criminal record a mile long and because of that, no one would rent me a decent place to live, no matter my education, my laudable work in the community, my awards, and my goodwill mattered not. I had a record and that was that! Nevertheless, because of the love Jesus Christ has for me and winning the courage awards," kept me focus and full of hope. I had to make it. I had to make it for me. Winning the courage award meant a lot to me; it showed that people had faith in me, and my work.

On the night I received the SJCSPCA, I also received Courage Awards in Journalism from both, The Commonwealth of Massachusetts House of Representative and the Boston City Council. Being in authority over my life for the first time, in my life, for the rest of my life has allowed me to live a calmer more productive, offspring peaceful, and spiritual life, in "my" new comfortable condominium lookalike apartment, on the Roxbury/Jamaica plain border near Franklin Park, an emerald garden of Olmsted. The ferocious ride on the rapids of my life did leave me pretty well scared up. Nevertheless, on that same rough ride, I'd also learned an encyclopedia worthy of wisdom, knowledge, and understanding.